the Andrew PARADIGM

the Andrew Paradigm

How to Be a
Lead Follower of Jesus

Michael J. Coyner

Abingdon Press
Nashville

THE ANDREW PARADIGM
HOW TO BE A LEAD FOLLOWER OF JESUS

Copyright © 2012 by Abingdon Press

This book is printed on acid-free paper.

Library of Congress Cataloging-in-Publication Data

Coyner, Michael J.
  The Andrew paradigm : how to be a lead follower of Jesus / Michael J. Coyner.
    p. cm.
  ISBN 978-1-4267-4338-2 (book - pbk. / trade pbk. : alk. paper)   1. Christian leadership.   2. Leadership—Religious aspects—Christianity.   3. Andrew, Apostle, Saint.
I. Title.
  BV652.1.C695 2012
  253—dc23

2012022737

12 13 14 15 16 17 18 19 20 21—10 9 8 7 6 5 4 3 2 1
MANUFACTURED IN THE UNITED STATES OF AMERICA

To the memory of my mother, Nina Jean Coyner,

who taught me so much about being a follower of Jesus and a leader

contents

Contents

intRoduction

Being a Lead Follower

During my childhood we often played the game "Follow the Leader." We took turns leading a line of children around the neighborhood. Sometimes we were the leader, but much of the time we were one of the followers. The simple childhood game taught us that being a good leader is related to being a good follower.

The concept of leading and following is relevant for the Christian leader today. Although there are many excellent books and websites and blogs about being a Christian leader, I find that few of them talk about this important lesson: being a better leader begins with being a better follower of Jesus.

This book is about following and leading. It is a study of those who were not quite ready to follow Jesus and a study of the disciple Andrew as a model of being a good and faithful follower of Jesus. It includes material to guide anyone who wants to improve his or her follower and leader skills.

One of the pastors in the Indiana Area of The United Methodist Church, where I serve as bishop, has developed a wonderful title for his role as pastor. He calls himself "Lead Follower" as a way of reminding himself and others that his most important role is being a follower of Christ, and among his church members he is a leader who leads from the position of being the Lead Follower. The Reverend Tony Johnson gave me permission to share his title and to use it as the title of this book because he affirms my efforts to write about leadership based on being a good follower.

This term *Lead Follower* is more than mere semantics, and it is certainly more than just a cute way to write something new about leadership. The term represents a shift in thinking from some of the writings about leadership popular in the American culture and in the church. These writings call for a leader who will take over, direct the future, cast the vision, and attract the faithful to a new mission or purpose. Somehow if we can just find this type of new leader, some seem to believe, then all will be right again with the church. Or as one of my colleague bishops has often said to me, "Leadership, leadership, leadership. It is all about leadership."

Is that true? Does the church or the business or the nation simply need to find an amazing leader who will solve all of our problems? Or is leadership something more? The desire for a leader to come to our rescue sounds eerily reminiscent of the desire of the Israelites for a king, so that they could be like every other nation (1 Samuel 8:1-9). Samuel warned them that having a king might become a distraction from following the Lord God as their King of kings. The people insisted, so God reluctantly gave them King Saul. He and the many other kings who succeeded Saul had some great leadership qualities, but they often lost their sense of direction by forgetting to be good followers of the lordship of God. The people suffered the results of that kind of leadership.

A Different Perspective on Leadership: The "Dance" of Leader/Follower

We always need good leaders, new leaders, and talented leaders, but we also need leaders who know how and when to be good followers. In every group and in every leadership team, leadership is a shared experience, a kind of "dance" between those times when one serves as the leader and when that same one is called to serve as an excellent follower.

How does this dance work? It begins with persons who are willing to be leaders, but their leadership must be granted, empowered, and authorized by the followers of the leader. One of the biggest mistakes I see young clergy make is going into their first pastoral experience thinking that being educated, ordained or licensed, and appointed or hired by a congregation grants them the authority to be a leader. Although some congregations and members initially will give a new pastor the benefit of the doubt, over time a pastor's leadership has to be earned, proved, and approved.

The same is true for laypersons elected to serve as chair of a ministry team or committee. Most of the other members of that group will give a new chair some initial respect and authority, especially if they are a healthy group, but that group will need to "bless" and accept their new leader if anything is going to be accomplished in the long run.

If there ever was a time when a certificate or a title meant a leader automatically had followers, that time is over. Leadership must be granted, earned, and supported by those who are willing to be followers. More than that, leadership is never just a one-way experience. Leadership is a product of the group, team, committee, or congregation. Leadership is shared; it is a give-and-take experience, a dance in which every member of the group takes a turn leading or facilitating. Leaders who assume that they do all the leading are either naive or ineffective. Leaders who listen, share, invite, trust, and connect with their followers are able to raise the level of effectiveness of the whole team.

The leadership team for the Indiana Conference, for example, is built around the concept that everyone is an expert in his or her own area of work. So when that person is leading part of a meeting or part of a project in which his or her expertise is paramount, then that person must be allowed by others to be the leader. The rest of the group must learn the fine art of followership.

I have learned during sixteen years of service as a bishop in The United Methodist Church that my real "authority" does not come from the outward symbols or the power of the office of bishop. There is a certain amount of respect for the office of bishop that I inherit in any setting, but real leadership comes from the willingness and the ability to work with groups, to share leadership, and to serve the mission of the church. When I remember the true source of my authority, I am a more effective leader; when I fall back upon the duties of the office for authority, my leadership suffers and so does the church I seek to serve. I have some authority and power that are granted to me by my election and consecration as a bishop, and of course our *Book of Discipline* gives me certain duties to perform. However, my real leadership comes from my efforts to build trust, to demonstrate my availability to people, and to prove that I am seeking to be a follower of Jesus.

Leading Like a Follower of Jesus: The Andrew Paradigm

For Christian leaders, leadership arises from our willingness to follow the One who leads us. We are called to put aside our own leadership desires and ambitions in order to be subordinate to the ultimate leadership of Christ. Excellent Christian leadership is more about following Jesus than it is about learning the latest fads or tricks from business, the marketplace, or the academy. Being an excellent Christian leader involves first and foremost being an excellent and faithful follower of Jesus Christ. The disciple Andrew is our model and the paradigm for being a Lead Follower.

How to Use This Book

This book moves from exploring "almost followers of Jesus" to examining Andrew as a model disciple and then to explicitly defining the characteristics of a Lead Follower. The book is designed for pastors and lay leaders, for personal reflection or a short-term study by a Sunday school class or any other group that lends itself well to a twelve-week study. It is designed to be a guide for a discussion of leadership issues, perhaps even a devotional study for church committees or council.

My intention is to provide a convenient and readable book about the issues of being a good follower and a good leader and finding the appropriate balance in our leader/follower roles on any Christian team.

Each chapter of the book contains discussion questions. These questions are developed from the inquiries of Jesus. Many have observed that one of the qualities of good leadership is asking the kinds of questions that help followers think, reflect, learn, and act. In fact, Ronald Heifetz has reminded us that the nature of leadership is not about providing easy answers but rather about asking the right questions to help the group discover its own answers (*Leadership Without Easy Answers* [Cambridge, Mass.: Belknap/Harvard University Press, 1994]). Jesus is certainly a model of such inquiries, and perhaps we have missed this quality because of our misplaced desire for leaders who provide easy answers. The discussion questions in this book begin with one of the inquiries of Jesus, followed by a response from one of the Lead Followers who serve as clergy or lay leaders in the Indiana Conference of The United Methodist Church.

An Inquiry from Jesus

Jesus asked his disciples, "Why are you afraid, you people of weak faith?" (Matt. 8:26). The situation for this inquiry was a time when he and his disciples were tossed and thrown about in a storm on the Sea of Galilee. Jesus slept peacefully through the entire emergency (talk about being a nonanxious presence!), until his disciples awakened him to save them. Before calming the storm, Jesus asked them this penetrating question about courage and faith. Were they ready to be his followers? If they could not handle a storm on the lake, how could they be ready for the more difficult tasks they would face as leaders in the kingdom of God? Jesus was training them as his followers, but he was anticipating their need to be leaders too. His question leads us to explore our own courage to be a leader and a follower.

The Response of a Lead Follower

Tony Johnson is the pastor of a new church in Johnson County, Indiana. He uses the term *Lead Follower* in his church newsletters to describe his role as a pastor. Tony answers:

Who does this? Who falls asleep in the midst of a storm that is bad enough to make a bunch of fishermen fear for their lives? Jesus does. And, at times, I feel like he does it in my life too. As a leader of a new church, in my marriage, in my family, and in my community, I sometimes feel like the disciples: sitting in a violently rocking boat, seemingly about to sink to the dark depths below. Sometimes that is what leadership is like—leadership that is not preceded by followership.

It was not the thunder and lightning that woke Jesus. He did not rise from his slumber because of the water that was surely crashing over him. (It was coming into the boat!) He did not awake as the tossing of the watercraft threw him from side to side. The storm did not wake Jesus and spring him to action. The pleas of his followers did.

When we lead on our own power, we are just bailing water, trying to stay afloat in the midst of the storm. However, when we are able to lead by first following Jesus, when we are able to lead out of a close connection and relationship with Jesus, when we are able to lead in all things by submitting our worldly leadership to our eternal followership of our Lord and Savior, then will we truly be able to be the leaders that God has called us to be.

On my own, I can only lead people to places I can create. As a follower of Jesus Christ, I can lead people to places that only he can create. The people I lead deserve the latter. You deserve the latter. I deserve the latter. That is why I am a Lead Follower.

Reflect and Discuss

1. How does your concept of "leadership" include or not include the need to be a good follower?

2. Do you ever find it difficult to allow others to lead? How and in what situations?

3. Is Jesus more of an "answer man" or someone who challenges with tough questions? Why?

4. How have you found your ability to follow tested in the midst of the storms of life?

5. Do you want to learn more about being a Lead Follower of Jesus?

PART I
the "Almost" Followers of Christ

John Wesley preached the sermon "The Almost Christian" before the university community on July 25, 1741 at St. Mary's in Oxford. He preached from Acts 26:28: "Almost thou persuadest me to be a Christian" (KJV). In his sermon, which became famous and one of the reasons Wesley was banned from preaching in many of the congregations of the Church of England, Wesley reminded his hearers that we are called to be more than just Christians in name, but rather to become what he called "altogether Christian."

In particular, Wesley argued that it is not good enough to try to be religious or to obey the rules of the Christian life just to avoid being sinful. It is not enough to be a good person, perhaps even a churchgoing person, without living by a deeper faith that goes beyond outward appearances. Wesley called his hearers—and surely the message is true for us today—to move from being "almost" to "altogether" Christians.

Likewise the Gospels make it clear that there were some persons who "almost" followed Jesus but were unable or unwilling to do so. In part I we look at four of these stories as a way of learning about the hindrances to our own faithful discipleship. We can't be a Lead Follower if we fail to be a follower of Jesus, so let's learn from these "almost followers" of Christ.

An Inquiry from Jesus

"If one of you wanted to build a tower, wouldn't you first sit down and calculate the cost, to determine whether you would have enough money to complete it?" (Luke 14:28).

Jesus warned his potential followers. His question pointed to the demands of being a disciple, and his question was a part of his teaching about the challenges that would come to his followers.

The Response of a Lead Follower

Ben Boruff is a young-adult leader who was one of the youngest persons ever elected to General Conference. Ben says:

A friend once asked me why I am a Christian. I struggled to reply. My mind pictured church-related items such as pews and praise bands, but none of those things helped me explain why I am a Christian. There are many personal and theological reasons why I call myself a Christian, but at that moment I could only think of hymnals and acolyte sticks. I later wondered, "If I am really a Christian, shouldn't Jesus Christ have immediately come to mind?"

Following Jesus requires intentionality. One of the biggest gifts my parents gave me was the opportunity thoughtfully and intentionally to consider Jesus. They allowed me to explore the challenges of being a disciple and decide if I wanted to follow Christ. The life of a disciple is not easy, as Jesus often illustrates, and following Christ is a commitment that demands our love and humility. The thought and attention I gave to the decision allowed me to enter into an intentional relationship with Christ.

My decision to follow Christ, however, did not end my spiritual struggles. As I discovered when my friend questioned my faith, I still forget sometimes what it means to be a Christian. Christianity is more than traditions and Sunday mornings, and a Christian is more than a decent person. It is easy to overlook the profound challenges that Jesus gave to his followers. Being a disciple is more than being good: it is about searching for perfection through the love of Jesus Christ.

Reflect and Discuss

1. As we move into these four stories of the "almost" followers of Christ, what parallels will you find to your own lukewarm discipleship?

2. Are you already "altogether" following Jesus? Why or why not?

3. How would John Wesley's sermon be received in your congregation?

4. Is it more difficult to be a follower of Jesus today than it was in Jesus' day? Is it more difficult today than it was in England in John Wesley's day?

5. How can we know whether we are "almost Christians" or "altogether Christians"?

Chapter One

POSSESSIONS CAN GET IN OUR WAY (MARK 10:17-22)

Mark 10 tells a sad story of a rich young man who could not leave his possessions behind in order to follow Jesus. Any fair reading of this story leads us to wonder what might have happened if he could have answered differently. It is apparent that he had qualities Jesus was seeking, perhaps the qualities that would have made him a key follower and eventually a key leader in the Christian movement. It is clear that Jesus cared for him. One translation says of Jesus that his "heart warmed towards him" (Mark 10:21 JBP). All of which makes it even sadder to note that we don't even know the name of this potential disciple. He could have become a Peter, James, John, or Andrew; but instead he walks away in silence, nameless, and remembered only for his inability to follow Jesus.

How might this nameless man have responded to Jesus when Jesus challenged him to sell all of his possessions, to give them away, and to come and follow along as a disciple? What if the young man had said, "You got me, Jesus. I have been trying so hard to keep all of the commandments of Moses, but I have overlooked my obsession with possessions. Will you help me overcome this?" I have to believe that Jesus would have welcomed the young man to come along and learn by following. Or what if the young man had said, "I always thought that my possessions were a sign of God's blessing and approval. Help me understand, Lord." Again, I would see Jesus embracing him like he did tax collectors and sinners. If only the young man could have admitted his obsession with his possessions and responded differently to Jesus. Perhaps he would have become a Lead Follower of Jesus.

Our Possessions Can Possess Us

What about us? Do we realize how easily our possessions can possess us? It is insidious, really. We get caught in a vicious cycle of wants that become needs and rights that become demands. What once was a nice little splurge

3

or a bonus or an unnecessary but enjoyable option can become an essential, or something we "must have." I notice how many "options" on our cars have become "standard" expectations. The first time I owned a car with variable-speed windshield wipers, it seemed like an extravagance. Now it seems as though I have to have that option—no longer as an option or a nice extra, but as an expectation. Some writers have called this "lifestyle creep" as a way of describing the reality that our expenses seem always to rise to the level of our income (or beyond).

Many couples struggling with unhappy marriages make a statement similar to this: "When we were first married, we were so happy, even though we had almost nothing. It seemed as though we had to work together and rely on each other just to get by, but it was fun. Now we are so busy with the big house or the bills or the vacation place, that we both work extra hours to make more money for our lifestyle. We've lost that sense of joy." What has happened? Possessions, lifestyle, and "success" have become enslaving. Somehow possessions that seemed so nice become a dominating influence in our lives, and we are unsatisfied. We have to have a bigger one, a better one, a nicer one, a newer one. It is a never-ending process of greed. Many have noted that, "Enough is always just a little bit more."

Even good things—like the books in my study—can become an obsession. I realized a few years ago that my own books had become a trophy case of my proven literacy rather than a resource to help my ministry and my discipleship. I now remember with some embarrassment how many moves from one ministry assignment to another have been burdened—literally—by the weight of all those books. Why? Was I really going to read those books over and over again? Was I really going to use those books for sermon preparation or Bible study or personal devotion? In some cases the answer could be yes, but most of those books were possessions that had started to possess and control my life.

Here is the lesson of our possessions: any good thing can become an obsession when it starts to dominate our life, control our attention, or distract us from our purpose and mission.

Generosity Is the Antidote to Greed

How can we prevent our possessions from possessing us? Jesus named it: give them away. Only a generous spirit can prevent us from being possessed by our possessions. So I made the painful choice a few years ago to give away most of my books. I shared them with younger clergy, I gave them to a bookstore, and I found other ways to share some with special friends. My effort to give away those books was serendipitous, in that I rediscovered some old favorite books on my shelf that I really did want to read again. What's more, I found a sense of freedom and joy from giving away many, many boxes of books. As I gave away those books, any sense of sadness or loss quickly turned into feelings of relief, joy, and energy.

I have tried to learn from that experience by developing a related policy for our household. My wife and I have agreed—and practiced for several years—to adopt the policy that whenever we purchase any new item for our household, we immediately give away a similar item to someone who needs it. In fact, Marsha has become a steady volunteer for a mission group called Second Starts, which collects household items to give to persons who are getting a second start in establishing a household. Some of those persons have been homeless, some are getting out of jail, and others have lost their possessions through floods and fires. No matter what the situation, her Second Starts group helps them get a new start in life. The bonus for us is that we have an automatic place to give away our possessions and to help others. We have shared that story with friends, and we find that people are constantly giving us their unused, nearly new, or excess possessions in order to help others get a second start.

There is a sense of joy, freedom, relief, and energy when we give away our possessions rather than allowing those same possessions to possess us.

Churches Possessed by Possessions

Even churches can become possessed by their possessions—their buildings, their endowed funds, their property, their history, their traditions, and their wealth. It is amazing how easily our church possessions can take over our mission and purpose, to the extent that many congregations slip into a focus upon "survival" as their only real mission. As with individuals, this is an insidious process. A new congregation can get along for several years with rented facilities, a shoestring budget, lots of volunteer staff (and very few paid positions), and even shared resources with a school or other congregation. Oftentimes these are the most productive years in the life of a church, in terms of reaching out in mission, making new disciples, and affecting lives.

Over the years the new congregation becomes "settled" into their own building. Much of the budget is diverted to paying the mortgage, rules are adopted to protect the property (it is always a telltale sign when I walk into a church facility and see more "Do Not" rules posted than messages of welcome), investments are protected, little memorial tags are placed on all the furniture, and much of the focus of church meetings revolves around possessions. It often is a slow process, but the result is a congregation that is focused upon itself, keeping its own members satisfied, and avoiding any risky outreach to others. It is an insidious process for a congregation, just as it is for an individual. Our possessions start to possess us.

What is the antidote for congregations trapped in that process? It is generosity; it is giving away our possessions. Many congregations have found freedom and new life by giving away their possessions. That can take many forms: sharing their facility with another congregation, perhaps a new church or that of a different ethnic group; launching a group of their own members to start a new ministry beyond the walls of the home church; giving a tithe (10 percent) or other percentage of their capital funds to mission projects around the world; partnering with a "sister congregation" in a poorer part of the city, state, or another country to share resources and also to receive witnesses from those other congregations; or even adopting policies to maintain only a minimum of reserves and resources, which allows for giving and sharing their surplus.

One congregation has adopted a policy of minimal reserves, and the church council meeting each January has become a joyous time of choosing mission projects to which they will give their excess funds after the books are closed at year-end. Since moving to this policy, the congregation has always had excess funds at year-end. People are attracted to a church that is serious about its generosity.

I wonder how Jesus would respond if our congregations stood before Jesus and asked, "What must we do to find life?" Would Jesus point to our possessions, our buildings, our endowed funds, and our rich heritage and challenge us to give it away?

Once, while attending a special service to dedicate a new church facility (something I do often in my role as a bishop), I saw the brave pastor stand on the front steps of the new sanctuary and pour a glass of red juice on the new carpet. His point was that our church buildings are not museums and that they are meant to get dirty with use. He said, "We should never care more about our new carpet than we do about the little child who spills on it." Perhaps his demonstration was excessive (and many of his members told him so that day), but his point was right. If our buildings possess us and consume our ministry attention, then we need to hear the invitation of Jesus to give it all away and to come and follow him.

Possessions Lead to Preferences Not Purpose

One of the most unnoticed aspects of our possessions is that they lead us to focus on our own personal preferences rather than on our God-given purpose in life. There are two choices in life: to live according to our own preferences, wants, needs, desires, and intentions or to live according to a plan, purpose, direction, and mission. Or to put it more bluntly, we can be self-centered and self-directed or God-centered and other-directed.

Our possessions lead us toward being focused upon our own preferences. Slowly but surely we focus our lives toward what we want, what we wish to purchase, what we want to protect, and what we desire. Our sense of purpose and mission gets lost in the midst of the allure of security and happiness from things, and even worse, from our own preferences about things. Even in the church, we start focusing upon what we want: what type of music, what color of carpet, what kinds of budget projects, or what style of staff. Slowly but surely our possessions lead us to believe this is "my church" and "my pastor" and "my people." We become more and more of an audience watching (and criticizing) the performance of the pastor, staff, music team, and church structure. Instead of seeing ourselves as disciples, we see ourselves as customers who demand more and more from "our church." Any sense of purpose is lost in favor of seeking our own preferences. Our possessions have taken complete possession of us, even our direction in life.

What About Us?

If we are going to be followers of Jesus, and if we are going to be leaders among his disciples, what possessions and preferences are hindering us?

It is easy to stand alongside the rich young man and to say to Jesus, "I am a good person. I try hard to obey all of the Christian principles. I attend church regularly, and I give a percentage of my income to the ministry of the church. Everyone who knows me would say I am a key leader in my church. I teach Sunday school, and I serve on a lot of committees. My family gives to the Thanksgiving and Christmas offerings. I sing the hymns and praise songs. I read the prayers in the liturgy, and I pray at home and on my own. I read the Bible, and I want to be a follower of Christ and a leader among his people." It is easy to stand there and to make those statements, but it may be hard to hear Jesus tell us that we are "almost disciples." It may be very difficult to hear Jesus say that "one more thing" is needed, especially if that "one more thing" is to get rid of those possessions that possess us.

Why is it that Jesus seems so harsh about possessions? Why are so many of his teachings directed against those who are rich? Why does he offer such encouragement to those who are poor? The story of the rich young man seems to make it clear that the issue is not our wealth or possessions. The issue is our trust, our faith, and our confidence. Possessions are insidious because they make the false claim of security. Possessions are a hindrance because they prevent us from putting our whole trust in God. Possessions cloud our judgment by convincing us that we are okay, that we have it together, and that we are self-sufficient. At least when we are poor, are living on a limited budget, or are getting along with very little, then we know we are dependent upon God.

Possessions can hinder us as followers of Jesus, and possessions can distract us from our invitation to be a Lead Follower.

An Inquiry from Jesus

"Why do you break the command of God by keeping the rules handed down to you?" (Matt. 15:3).

Jesus warned the religious leaders of his day. His warning was addressed to those who kept religious rules but avoided the deeper issues of faith and trust. Trusting Jesus, not merely keeping the religious rules, is the deeper issue. A person can attend worship, pledge to the church, attend meetings, and meet all of the "requirements" of being religious, yet she or he can still miss the point of trusting in God's grace.

The Response of a Lead Follower

Frank Beard is Superintendent of the North Central District in the Indiana Conference and also is a key leader within the denomination. He serves as Secretary for the General Board of Discipleship (GBOD) in Nashville, Tennessee, and he is a member of the Commission on General Conference planning team, in which he serves as the head of the program committee. He also serves on the North Central Jurisdictional Episcopacy Committee, and he was elected as a clergy delegate to the 2012 General Conference and led the Indiana delegation. Frank says:

> The sign on the counter in the gift shop simply read, "In God We Trust. All Others Pay Cash!" The cute sign was a twist on the popular currency motto, "In God We Trust." Another adaptation exchanges "God" with "Got." The rich young ruler appears to be one of those who would, at least by his outward action, give approval to the sentiment, "In Got We Trust."

The rich young ruler became distracted by his possessions and failed the crucial test of submission and surrender. His attachment to possessions caused him to forsake his kneeling posture. The challenge by Jesus to wed legalism, the second half of the Ten Commandments, with unbridled loyalty, the first half of the Commandments, caused the rich young ruler to abandon his quest for eternal life.

One of the tests that I use to help stay on the path of surrender is the "John the Baptist" test. When John was confronted with his decline in popularity and Jesus' rise in notoriety, John's response was, "He [Jesus] must increase and I must decrease" (John 3:30). Lead Followers are called to forsake self in order to advance the cause of Christ. Following Christ is not about "me." I love the challenge in Judson W. Van DeVenter's classic song:

All to Jesus I surrender; Humbly at His feet I bow,

Worldly pleasures all forsaken; Take me, Jesus, take me now

I surrender all, I surrender all; All to Thee, my blessed Savior, I surrender all.

Lead followers are called to arise from the altar of surrender with a greater determination to be totally yielded to Christ.

Reflect and Discuss

1. Which possessions are your most treasured? Is their value monetary or something else?

2. How much time do you spend worrying about your financial "security"?

3. Have you discovered the joy of giving? Have you ever discovered the freedom of extravagant giving? Why or why not?

4. Is your congregation more concerned about the "rules" of behavior for your building, your property, and your budget than about the Golden Rule of Jesus?

5. Is your congregation focused inwardly on preferences or outwardly on purpose? How can you lead your congregation to be freed from possessions?

Chapter Two

UNRESOLVED GRIEF CAN HOLD US BACK (LUKE 9:59-60)

One of the harshest responses from Jesus to an "almost follower" was to the one who said, "Let me first go and bury my father." Jesus responded with, "Let the dead bury the dead." His response seems uncaring, insensitive, and even rude.

What could Jesus have meant? Biblical scholars suggest two likely possibilities, and both have to do with the Jewish customs of the day. The first possibility is that the person was talking about the typical process of taking care of an elderly parent, all the way to death. It involved selling off the parental properties, taking the parent into one's household, and providing for the parent's care in his or her waning years. Obviously such a process could take a few years or many years, just as it would in our day. So Jesus may have said, "You can't use that excuse to put your life and your calling on hold. Now is the time to respond to the kingdom of God and to my invitation to be a disciple."

An even more likely possibility is that the person was involved in the lengthy Jewish process of grieving after the death of a loved one. Depending upon the person's adherence to various rabbinical traditions, that grief process could continue for many months. In this possibility, Jesus is saying to the person, "It has been long enough. It is time to move on from your grief and your mourning process. Come and follow me and get back to life again."

Either possibility can still sound harsh and perhaps even indifferent. Modern understandings of grief concur that unresolved grief can hold us back from fully living and responding to a higher calling in our lives. Jesus is apparently saying to this "almost disciple" that grief can freeze us and prevent us from moving on.

The Grief Process

Elisabeth Kübler-Ross first identified the stages of grief: denial, anger, bargaining, depression, and acceptance (*On Death & Dying* [New York:

Scribner, 1969]). Although her study was originally an effort to help dying patients deal with the reality of impending death, her understanding of grief illustrates how grief is a process with many steps, not necessarily in a straight line, through which we must move toward acceptance.

With this understanding of the grief process as a background to our Bible story, it may become even more apparent what Jesus meant by his challenge to "let the dead bury the dead." As was the case with many others whom Jesus healed, Jesus may have seen the pain and heartache of unresolved grief and offered healing. Grief is real, the grief process can be long and involved, and those who are stuck in the process may need help moving on.

Moving on to acceptance is not easy. In the past two years my wife and I have grieved the death of both of her parents, my own mother, and several close friends and colleagues. Such grief can be paralyzing in many ways. It cannot be hurried, but it must include progress, ever so slowly, to move on to resolution. It is all too easy to become stymied in that process, and a person—any person—needs help moving on toward acceptance, resolution, and peace.

Did Jesus see the need for a grieving person to let go of his unresolved grief in order to follow and be a disciple? Apparently so. Does Jesus see our grief today and also want to help us heal and move on? I believe the answer is yes. How else do we explain the several cases in which Jesus asked persons if they wanted to be helped and healed? In such cases it seems that Jesus wanted persons to be healed and not just cured. To be cured is to have the condition or affliction removed, like getting over a virus. To be healed may include being cured, but it involves the deeper issues of learning to accept and forgive and resolve our ailments, whether we are cured or not.

One of my dear friends lost two of her three teenage children to different accidents many years ago. When I met her years later, she obviously had found her way to acceptance and peace. So I asked her, rather foolishly, "How do you get over something like that?" She responded with the wisdom of a long journey through grief: "You don't get over it. You get used to it, and you get on with life." Her words taught me that grief is not something from which we should be cured; rather it is a hurting love that needs to be healed. She was also helpful to many people who came to her in their own grief to ask for help in moving forward. On more than one occasion I heard her tell someone in grief, "You can get through this. It will take time, but one of these days you will put away your tissues and get back to living your life." She helped people get adjusted to what she called "the new normal" in their lives. Can we see Jesus wanting to help someone with that kind of healing, in order to get used to the loss and also to move on with life and become a disciple?

Grief is painful, and yet it is also the backside of our love, so it is not something to be cured. Only those who never love can escape the pain of grief. We grieve because we have loved, but sometimes we forget that love as we get lost in our own pain. Sometimes it takes a shocking statement—such as "Let the dead bury the dead"—to help us realize we are stuck in the grief process and hamstrung by our unresolved grief. Being confronted with grief can help us break through to the love that is the heart of our grief and thus help us find healing for a situation that cannot be cured.

Our unresolved grief needs healing, and it can keep us from being a full and complete follower of Jesus. Likewise, a leader dealing with his or her own grief is less able to be a Lead Follower. Until we get used to our new normal and get on with life, it is very difficult to follow Jesus completely.

Congregations and Unresolved Grief

Congregations, too, can be overwhelmed with lingering grief over the loss of a beloved pastor to retirement, death, or simply moving away. At such times, many in the congregation discover, sadly, that they were "almost Christians" who actually were just fans of a pastoral leader. In these instances it can be nearly impossible for the next pastoral leader to gain trust and empowerment to lead. Until the unresolved grief over a previous pastor is healed, the new pastor cannot offer a cure. Attempts by the new pastor to lead can be met with irrational resistance. Often the new pastor is accused of not being a competent leader, even though the real issue is unresolved grief that keeps a congregation stuck in the past.

Sometimes the departing pastor unintentionally sets up the successor for such failure. Too many departing pastors want to avoid their own issues of grief, so they refuse to participate fully in the various good-byes that a congregation wants to offer at the time of their retirement or their move to a new ministry. Several books, including my own, *Making a Good Move,* (Nashville: Abingdon Press, 2000), have pointed to the need to "leave well," which means allowing the natural grief process to move forward. Failing to allow this grief to be named, experienced, and celebrated with various good-bye ceremonies can interfere with the congregation's need to grieve and can actually prevent the incoming pastor from having a good ministry. Such unresolved grief needs to be healed.

Other congregations deal with unresolved grief over a more glorious past, or at least their perception of a more glorious past. Thomas Friedman says, "When a group has more memories than dreams, then it has no future" (*The World is Flat: A Brief History of the Twenty-first Century* [New York: Farrar, Straus and Giroux, 2005]. p. 451). Too many congregations live with unresolved grief over the loss of a past, which prevents them from dreaming and attaining a new future. One can only wonder how many of these congregations have planned retreats, hired consultants, studied their own communities, and engaged in a variety of attempts to move to the future, only to find those efforts failing because they did not accept the healing of their unresolved grief that is offered by being followers of Jesus.

A few years ago I watched a church consultant handle well the unresolved grief of a congregation whose previous history had indeed been glorious. Worship attendance had declined over the years from an average of 2,000 to 400. The consultant displayed a graph of their attendance history; next to it was the graph of a new congregation that had grown to 400 in worship attendance during its first five years. He asked the question, "Since both congregations have 400 in attendance, what makes the difference in their attitude about that identical mathematical number?" People quickly responded, saying, "What a great church we used to be." The consultant then covered up the statistics of the past years for both congregations and asked, "What would it take to live without that baggage of the past hanging over you?" A wonderful discussion followed, much hurt was expressed, and the grief was named. That congregation began to make plans for a new future by facing up to the grief of a lost past.

Grief Can Be Healed

While grieving for my mother, I found comfort in a sympathy card that read, "Everything will be okay in the end. If it is not okay, then it's not the end." That card helped me look forward to the grieving process being over— or at least moving on to the acceptance stage—in order to find the healing that makes things "okay." It took time, but it happened.

I know one congregation that was stuck in unresolved grief over a previous, beloved pastor who had refused to allow the usual good-bye events. He had thought he was helping the church "rise above such silliness." Consequently the congregation was dealing with unresolved grief through several brief and unsuccessful pastorates. A subsequent pastor diagnosed the situation as unresolved grief and invited the beloved predecessor to come back and preach and be honored as a "pastor emeritus." After having time to express their proper good-byes and appreciations to the beloved pastor, the congregation was healed of their unresolved grief and was ready to move forward under the wise leadership of their current pastor.

Jesus invites us to be healed from whatever grief is holding us back. He does not ask us to forget it, get over it, or pretend it is not real. He does invite us to discover the power and relief that come from healing. Unresolved grief can hold us back from being a follower and a Lead Follower. Being healed of such grief—no matter what the cause—can free us to follow and to lead.

An Inquiry from Jesus

"Do you want to get well?" (John 5:6).

Jesus is prepared to offer healing, but first he asks a tough question to the man waiting beside the pool of Bethsaida. The man responds with a list of excuses about being unable to get into the water in time to be healed, and it is obvious that he has been living out those excuses for many years. Jesus moves to the heart of the matter by inquiring, "Do you want to get well?" and then he offers the healing the man has needed.

The Response of a Lead Follower

Susie Bloom is a mother whose son, Todd, died at the age of thirteen from a rare form of cancer. She has used that grief and loss to motivate her to offer ministry to others as a layperson. Here is her response:

My arms felt empty; no Todd to hug. A heaviness hung over me; I awoke every morning, crying. My grief was all consuming and felt like it would go on forever. And then, gradually, light began to shine again in my darkness. As I look back, I am thankful for all the ways God helped my desire to be healed. I remember especially these three:

• The body of Christ reached out to our family, offering fellowship and outings and sending books and cards. A friend took me to exercise class with her, and neighbors included my husband in their Bible study group. One friend even wrote my name on her calendar each week for two years so that she would not forget to reach out to me.

• My pastor offered me a volunteer job, helping new people get comfortable at our church. I discovered that helping others lessened my grief. I also started a grief support group, and together, with God's help, we moved toward healing.

- I went on an Emmaus retreat, and in that close fellowship time with God and loving Christians, I opened my heart to God's restoring joy.

It has been nineteen years since Todd died, and now when I think of him, it is with a thankful heart that he was in my life. I find that my experience has left me sensitive to those who are hurting, and it is my delight and privilege to reach out to them. I ask God to give me eyes to see beyond their "I'm fine."

It is a new concept for me to think about a whole congregation being in grief and pain. As I consider that concept, I know just where my compassion is needed now; I've seen their grief and am already praying, "God use me."

Reflect and Discuss

1. What unresolved grief are you carrying with you today?

2. Is the congregation, group, or organization you lead still dealing with grief from some past event? If so, what are the signs and indications of that unresolved grief?

3. What steps are you willing to take in order to be healed of your own grief or to lead your people to be healed of their grief?

4. Sometimes people are stuck in grief, and sometimes they don't want to be healed. What questions of inquiry can bring awareness to those persons? What is your role as a Lead Follower to ask such questions?

5. Do you want to get well?

Chapter Three

Family is important, but it can limit us (Luke 8:19-21)

One of the most shocking incidents in the life of Jesus as recorded in the Gospels is the story from Luke 8 in which Jesus rejects his family and claims his disciples as his new family. Even in our day and culture, this story appears shocking and quite a contrast to the typical assumption that the values of Jesus and the Christian community are equivalent with "family values" as defined by some religious and political groups. Far from following the expected mores of his day, Jesus turns away his family and challenges the typical notion of loyalty to one's family.

Why? All three of the Synoptic Gospels report this story, but only Mark records an earlier one that may explain the reason Jesus turns his family away. Mark reports a story from very early in Jesus' ministry, after he called his disciples and began his preaching, teaching, and healing: "Jesus entered a house. A crowd gathered again so that it was impossible for him and his followers even to eat. When his family heard what was happening, they came to take control of him. They were saying, 'He's out of his mind!'" (Mark 3:20-21).

Little wonder that Jesus later says that his true family is composed of those who hear and believe the truth. His own family, early in his ministry at least, seemed not to understand his mission, and they tried to take him home. Far from accepting their efforts to control him, Jesus differentiates himself, and he also later preaches that his message will turn a man against his father, a daughter against her mother, and daughter-in-law against her mother-in-law (Matt. 10:34-36). He also later says that the demands of being a disciple are so great that "those who love father or mother more than me aren't worthy of me.... Those who don't pick up their crosses and follow me aren't worthy of me. Those who find their lives will lose them, and those who lose their lives because of me will find them" (Matt. 10:37-39). Given those words from Jesus, it is obvious that his family—at least in this early time of his ministry—are at best "almost followers" who cannot quite understand him.

So was Jesus anti-family? Not at all. Later in the Gospels, as Jesus was dying upon the cross, he intentionally called upon his disciple John to treat Jesus' mother, Mary, like his own mother. Nor were the family of Jesus always opposed to him. Eventually we read that his brother James is a leader in the early church, along with his mother, Mary.

The Problem with Family

Jesus teaches us that family is important and valuable but can be limiting. A healthy family is one who does not smother its members but rather allows them to be individuals who do not always agree or stay under control. An unhealthy family can smother with love to the extent that no one can differentiate or become independent of the family system.

Edwin Friedman names different conditions of a family system. In his classic book *Generation to Generation,* along with many subsequent writings, Friedman helps us understand that "family" can be dysfunctional and unhealthy. In such a dysfunctional family, the individual members are "controlled"—just what the family of Jesus tried to do to him, as recorded in Mark 3. Variations are not accepted, outsiders are not welcome, and independent thinking is the cause of family distress. The family of Jesus, early in the Gospel story, shows all of these classic signs of being dysfunctional.

Jesus himself seems to demonstrate at an early age what Friedman calls the healthy position of "differentiation." In the only story we have about Jesus from his birth to his adulthood, we learn that Jesus (who was about twelve years old at the time) disobeyed his parents, left the caravan going home from Jerusalem back to Nazareth, and spent three additional days in the Temple discussing, learning, and questioning the elders. Even when his family finds him after a frantic search, his response is teenager-like: "Didn't you know I would be in my Father's house?" Such insolence is not welcome in most families. This story, too, puts into context the reasons for the later words of Jesus when he says that his true family is not his birth family. He claims a new, larger, more inclusive family of those who believe and respond to his ministry.

Families Can Smother—or Set Free

In our current culture, the emphasis on family can be either unhealthy or healthy. *Family* is a neutral term, not a value. It all depends upon what type of "family" one experiences.

As a pastor, I have watched some families smother their members with too much "family time"—even to the detriment of their professed Christian faith. I remember one family in particular who told me that they would be present "every Sunday" during the school year but not during the summer months when they would be "family camping." That seemed innocuous enough, even though I wondered why their understanding of "every Sunday" had such limits. However, I soon observed the smothering nature of their family. It was not long before I saw their teenage kids rebelling against that much family time, and not just the typical teenage efforts to differentiate. Their kids had to go to extremes in order to escape the smothering love of their family. Differentiation was not encouraged, and it became like an armed revolt. It was sad to counsel with the mother and father, who genuinely had tried to protect their kids from problems by imposing such a smothering family lifestyle. They simply could not understand why their kids had turned against them.

My own family of origin was less than perfect, but I was blessed to grow up in a Christian home in which we were encouraged to develop our own sense of independence and differentiation. That encouragement included part-time jobs for our own spending money (and the freedom to spend it as we chose), time to be with friends, and even traveling without parents. Most remarkably, I returned home from my freshman year in college to find that my old bedroom had been converted into a family den. There was a couch with a foldout bed and a closet to hang my clothes, but the message was clear. I was told by my parents, "There is always a place for you when you are home, but we know that you are growing up and starting to move on with your life. So we want to get more use out of your old bedroom." I remember feeling a bit surprised by that change, but I also remember feeling empowered and encouraged to become an adult.

What if your family of origin was dysfunctional and oppressive? Even more difficult, what if your family of origin was abusive or damaging? The model of Jesus and his own family would suggest: find a congregation of other disciples with whom you can relate and proceed to be Lead Followers in a healthier environment.

Church Is Not a "Family"

With the problems Jesus had with his own family, and with current understanding that some families are dysfunctional, it becomes apparent that we in the church must be very careful about our use of the term *family* to describe our Christian congregations. One reason for the need to be careful is simply the presence of so many different types of families in our culture in the United States. In fact, if one thinks of "family" as a father who works, a mother who stays home with the kids, and two or more school-age children, that type of family now represents a very small percentage of our U.S. households. Many other types of families are a part of any typical congregation. Church announcements about "family dinners" or other "family activities" may be perceived as quite exclusive by some persons. It is perhaps quite a learning experience for congregational leaders to examine their church Sunday bulletin, newsletter, websites, and e-mail to see how the term *family* may be used in ways that are smothering and limiting.

In fact, one could well argue that the term *family* is not a good description of a congregation, as in saying, "We just love our church family." That is not a term used in the New Testament for a gathering of Christians. The more normative term is *congregation* or *household* or *people of God*. Perhaps we have so many small and sometimes dysfunctional local congregations because they have been shaped by the culture of family in our secular world. Perhaps being a Lead Follower of Jesus involves expanding our understanding of *church* beyond the terminology of *family*. Perhaps Jesus was right to insist upon a wider and deeper understanding of *family* to include all who hear and respond to the good news of the gospel. Perhaps a focus upon inviting, welcoming, including, and involving all persons—regardless of their family configuration or their blood relationships—would help all congregations fulfill more completely the teachings of Jesus.

Interestingly, this passage from Luke is actually skipped or omitted from the *Common Lectionary* of Sunday scripture readings. Could it be that we find Jesus' words about family to be too difficult to follow? Could it be that we all need to struggle to expand our understanding of church beyond the category of family? If church is not limited by the term *family*, then church might become more of a place where Lead Followers are developed, nurtured, encouraged to risk, and welcomed as both Leaders and Followers of the Christian movement.

An Inquiry from Jesus

"What do you want?" (Matt. 20:21).

Jesus asked this of the mother of James and John when she approached him to seek special status for her sons. Given the background of Jesus' own family misunderstandings, it is not surprising that the mother of James and John misunderstood both the mission of Jesus and the calling her sons had accepted to be followers of Jesus. She certainly did not understand the concept of Lead Follower. No doubt this is not the only time that motherly love was misguided. Many of us have mothers who have been overly supportive, even interfering in our careers. But the question of Jesus is a good one for any family member: What do you want? Do you want to allow your child, parent, spouse, or relative to be free to follow Jesus? Or do you place other family expectations on those loved ones?

The Response of a Lead Follower

Jennifer Gallagher is a young mother of five, including two sets of twins, who also serves as Treasurer of the Indiana Conference of The United Methodist Church. Here is her response:

> My early faith development was based on traditionalism and obligation. "Showing up" at the church building for a weekly service and a catechism class, memorizing canned prayers, and regularly confessing my sins is a perhaps oversimplified summary. These early roots taught me a direct correlation between being a follower of Jesus and being "present" in a community of churchgoers. It is my roots that in turn give me wings because they leave me yearning for much more as an adult. The most profound influence on my faith today has been observing and experiencing the deep faith and witness of people in my life. Their obvious peace through faith is inspiring and keeps me always seeking and searching. Yet my roots influence that journey as I am pulled to seek and search in a church community rather than trying alone.
>
> The simple logistics of five children within a five-year span plus two full-time-working parents makes the concept of smothering difficult to imagine. That is not to say there isn't more than enough love shared among us. As parents, our goal is to instill independence with a strong sense of mutual support, tolerance for "messing up," and a good sense of humor. Most important, we try to be loving all the time, even when circumstances feel out of control. Many years ago during a period of high stress for me at work, my husband said to me, "Don't leave the best of you at work." He knew I was cordial, kind, and respectful at work but was not practicing that same patience at home with the people I love and who love me back. That comment has stuck with me for many years and reminds me the

best way to love my family is to give them the best of myself every day.

I hope the fulfillment I experience in leading a daily Christian life helps me recognize when I am straying from the path that Jesus wants. I have experienced a "show" of faith that leaves a feeling of emptiness. I believe loving my family without controlling or judging is the best way to model to them what this path brings to my life, so that rather than an obstacle to me they are observers who become inspired, as I have been inspired by others.

My husband and I want to nurture in our children a strong base for living a Christian life by modeling that life in everything we do, every day. This goes way beyond "showing up" at the church building once a week. I hope that we will yearn for substantive growth in our faith throughout our lives and find meaningful value in that process. I want to experience a true peace in faith in my life, a peace that I have seen in others and search for on my journey.

Reflect and Discuss

1. Was your family of origin helpful in giving you "wings" as well as "roots" for your faith?

2. In your current family alignment, how do you offer love without becoming smothering?

3. Is your congregation a place where all kinds of families are welcomed?

4. If your own family—past or present—becomes an obstacle to being a Lead Follower, can you choose to differentiate and to follow Jesus?

5. What do you want for your family and for yourself?

Chapter Four

SEEKERS DON'T ALWAYS BECOME FOLLOWERS (JOHN 18:33-38)

A lengthy conversation between Pontius Pilate and Jesus, as recorded in the Gospel of John, reveals someone who is seeking, unsure of his own values, unable to lead because he is trying to survey the popular opinions, and curious about this Jesus who speaks of truth. Pontius Pilate may not be the typical "seeker" whom many churches today are trying to reach, but he does represent another "almost follower" of Christ. Pilate illustrates that there is a big difference between seeking and following Jesus.

Pilate keeps trying to understand Jesus in the terms of his own secular world. He asks Jesus if he is a king. He wonders how Jesus fits into the context of the Jewish religious leaders who are accusing Jesus. He seems especially perplexed when Jesus talks about truth, and he offers the haunting question, "What is truth?" spoken like someone who yearns to know truth but who is not sure he would recognize it if he saw it.

Jesus and Various Seekers

Jesus encountered several persons who were seekers, looking for truth or perhaps for reassurance about their own ideas, and Jesus did not fall into the trap of trying to please them. In fact, he challenged them with his own certainty about his identity, his mission, and his clear focus on obeying God's will. Consider the following:

Nicodemus, the teacher of the law, comes to Jesus at night, seeking to understand Jesus. He gives Jesus credit for the good Jesus is doing but seems perplexed by Jesus' own self-understanding. Rather than engage in a philosophical conversation about his own mission, Jesus challenges Nicodemus to be "born anew" to the new insights of the kingdom of God. At this point in the narrative, Nicodemus could rightly be called an "almost follower" of Jesus, but there is evidence later that he started to become a defender of Jesus during his trial and even later a supporter who helps find a burial site for Jesus.

The rich young man, whom we have already considered in chapter 1 for the hindrance of his possessions, also begins his conversation with Jesus with the appellation of "Good Teacher" and a question about his own worthiness. Jesus quickly rebukes that approach by saying, "Why do you call me good? No one is good except the one God" (Mark 10:18). Jesus is not lured into the attempts to barter goodness with the young man who claimed he had obeyed all the laws since his youth.

Likewise Jesus refuses to become the arbiter of two brothers arguing over how to divide their parents' estate (Luke 12:14). Jesus simply refuses to respond to every need or to play games about being religious.

In Pilate's story, Jesus responds to Pilate's own wonderings about truth by simply asserting, "I am the truth." He pushes Pilate to make a choice, and Pilate chooses poorly and is remembered forever as the one who crucified the Savior of the world, even while declaring Jesus innocent. So much for seeking truth and following it!

Who Are the Seekers Today?

Many megachurches and even smaller churches are focused on reaching the "seekers" of our culture. Many congregations hold "seeker services"—worship services that attract and encourage seekers to attend. Although definitions vary, *seekers* are either persons who are "unchurched," or have never attended church regularly, or "dechurched," or used to be churchgoers but have been hurt or neglected by the church. Either way, they are persons seeking a new start with God, exploring the possibility of a congregation that is hospitable, and then moving forward—albeit slowly—toward a new or fresh understanding of the Christian faith. Although many assume seekers are young adults, actually there are seeking persons in every age group. Given that many church experts now estimate active churchgoers are an increasingly small percentage of the population (perhaps as low as 15 percent in some parts of the United States), one can understand the need for the church to find ways to include such seekers.

What do seekers want? Opinions vary, but most suggest that seekers are looking for welcome, love, and meaning. Congregations respond with worship services and facilities and programs to meet these needs. Often these include secular or familiar music, relevant messages that deal with real-life situations, and a lessening of traditional symbols, liturgy, and doctrine. Seekers, it is presumed, are like customers shopping at the mall who must be attracted and catered to, lest we lose them to the next seeker-friendly congregation down the street or across town.

Seeker-friendly pastors and congregations have moved services into auditoriums without any religious symbols, included videos to reach an audience used to learning more from images than from wordy propositions, and developed fast-paced worship events modeled after the children's television show *Sesame Street* in terms of repetition, short lessons, and attractive personalities. Such seeker-sensitive congregations have their critics, of course, who ask questions about lack of depth, the absence of calls to discipleship, and the danger of being entertainment-oriented and consumer-driven.

The difficulty of discerning the balance between offering hospitality and merely pleasing consumers is illustrated by a conversation I once overheard. A young woman was sharing how enthusiastic she was about her congregation and how she had invited many of her friends to come to her church and many had responded and come. Then she proceeded to explain that her "selling point" was to invite her friends by saying, "Come to our church because you can believe anything and still be a Christian." Really? Is that the model of invitation and hospitality we want? Are seekers really helped by that approach? Most important, does that approach follow the model of Jesus?

Jesus and the Seekers

The approach of Jesus to such "seekers" is both supportive of seeker-friendly congregations and also a helpful critique. The Gospels certainly portray Jesus as someone who welcomed interactions with everyone: small children, a Samaritan woman, a Roman commander, religious leaders, lepers, foreigners, and just about every category of person of his day. His model of hospitality affirms those congregations and Christian leaders who work to make the church today more available and open to all.

However, Jesus deals with seekers without catering to their whims or leaving them confident in their own misconceptions. He can seem firm, even harsh, in his response to some who seek to pull him into their worldview. He refuses to engage in their petty arguments or their differences with other people. He responds to questions, but often by asking deeper and more profound questions as his response. Jesus, above all, seems clear about his own personhood and mission, and thus he is undeterred by those who come to him seeking answers from their own agenda.

This example of Jesus should be a lesson for the church today. In the church today we need to be caring but stringent like Jesus in our approach to seekers. Our mission is not to engage persons in pleasant conversations about the truth or to welcome every effort to draw us into unrelated contentions about people's latest projects or concerns. It certainly is not our task to survey the market and try to meet the expectations of every consumer. Our mission and our focus are on inviting others to become followers of Jesus. The paradox of Jesus' interaction with seekers is that he accepted them and engaged them, and yet he also challenged them to a deeper faith. Even his use of parables to teach was a unique style that invited participation by his hearers. Jesus models for the church today an openness to fresh approaches of communication, even while challenging seekers to grow. A healthy congregation does not pander to the culture but leads seekers to become disciples of Jesus.

Our Personal Seeking

For all of us, this same warning about "seeking" holds true. We can disguise our own reluctance to follow Jesus by telling ourselves that we are seeking to be faithful, to know the truth, and to have the right agenda. Perhaps our claim to "seek" is really just another way of saying that we are "almost followers" of Jesus who have not yet made a commitment to be his disciples.

Theology is often defined as "faith seeking understanding." That is quite different from the seeker's motto, which according to the seekers who engaged Jesus seems to be, "I have to understand before I can have faith." Jesus invites persons to "come, follow me" and to trust that they (we) will learn along the way. If our seeking spirits must have all of our questions answered before we commit to discipleship, then we are working on our agenda and not the agenda of Jesus. The lesson of Jesus and the "seekers" of his day seems to be that we should not let our own seeking get in the way of our following Jesus.

Perhaps we need to hear once again the promise of Jesus to his followers that if we will seek, we will find. Following Jesus is the pathway to such finding, and it is also the training ground for becoming Lead Followers.

An Inquiry from Jesus

"Who do people say the Human One is?" (Matt. 16:13).

Pilate as a "seeker" is never able to move toward becoming a follower of Jesus, and so that story ends without an inquiry from Jesus. Perhaps we should not be too hard on Pilate, because he reflects the lack of understanding often displayed by Jesus' own disciples. However, in this passage from Matthew, Jesus leads his disciples in an amazing discussion about his identity and purpose. He starts by asking them about public-opinion polls. They respond with the poll results, that some said Jesus was John the Baptist, others Elijah, and others Jeremiah or one of the prophets. So far this is just a "seekers" discussion. Then Jesus moves the discussion to a personal-commitment level by asking, "And what about you? Who do you say that I am?" Of course we remember that it was Simon Peter, the impetuous one, who responds with the faith affirmation, "You are the Christ, the son of the living God!"

The inquiry of Jesus, "Who do you say I am?" is the question seekers and longtime Christians alike must answer. Otherwise we will just be the "almost followers" of Jesus.

The Response of a Lead Follower

The Reverend Mark Beeson is the senior pastor of Granger Community Church in South Bend, Indiana, one of the largest United Methodist congregations in the country. As the founding pastor in 1986, Mark had a dream and calling to reach those who were seeking answers but were turned off by traditional churches. Meeting for the first several years in a movie theater, Granger Church has a passion for helping persons answer the inquiry of Jesus. Here is Mark's response:

> God loves seekers. Jesus made clear the consequence of seeking first the kingdom of God. Seeking is not an end; it is the way of finding. Amos said, "Seek the LORD and live."
>
> The psalmist tells us, "The LORD looks down from heaven on all humanity to see if there are any who seek God." But John Wesley understood the Scriptures to be clear; total depravity means we are dead in our sins and cannot help ourselves. If God didn't preemptively move us, no one would ever seek at all. Salvation is impossible without a free and prior act of God.
>
> So, followers of Jesus thank God for the seekers, make room for the seekers, and create environments in their meetings for seekers to find the Lord. Services of worship aren't designed to veil what God has made plain; the Word became flesh and dwelt among us, and we beheld his glory. In other words, we got it. And we loved the One who first loved us.

Our gatherings—whether corporately on weekends or in smaller groups meeting from house-to-house—are attractive to seekers because we don't try to wrap the gospel in a cloak of otherworldly mystery; instead we lift up Jesus for all to see. We speak to those awakened by God in their language. We stride across cultural barriers to be with seekers. Following the example of our Lord, we take his light into the darkness. John identifies its essence as "the true light that gives light to all."

Ask yourself: what good comes from ignoring the seekers God has awakened and drawn to himself? Imagine what could happen if the church made plain the gospel and so beautifully embodied it that seekers were regularly confronted with the risen Lord, who required of them an answer to his question, "Who do you say that I am?"

Reflect and Discuss

1. How does your church keep a balance between offering hospitality and falling into the trap of consumerism?

2. In what ways does your congregation provide hospitality and "open space" for seekers to enter and begin to discover the demands of discipleship?

3. If it is true that not all seekers become followers, how can we help more seekers make that transition into discipleship?

4. How do you personally answer the question of Jesus, "Who do you say that I am?"

5. How did the church or your family or friends or a spiritual retreat help you find your answer to that question of Jesus?

PART II
the andrew paradigm of a lead follower

Now that we have considered some of the persons who were "almost followers" of Jesus, hopefully we have learned from their experiences the dangers and choices that can hold us back from being Lead Followers. Now consider the disciple Andrew and the ways in which he is a model of a follower of Jesus but also a model of being a Lead Follower.

Andrew is a favorite disciple for many people. Perhaps that is because Andrew is not a "big name" disciple, not Peter or James or John, who receive so much attention in the Gospels. We actually don't have many stories about Andrew, but those we have point to an "ordinary" disciple who models for us what faithful discipleship is all about. Even more, if we look carefully at the Gospel records, we find that Andrew was a Lead Follower who provided important, yet quiet, leadership behind the scenes.

The following chapters examine the model of Andrew in hopes that we can each better learn how to be a Lead Follower. It would be a wonderful affirmation for any of us to be considered an "Andrew" or "Andrea" in our own discipleship and leadership.

An Inquiry from Jesus

"How much bread do you have?" (Mark 8:5).

Jesus' disciples wondered how to feed a large crowd. As we will see in chapter 7, Andrew took Jesus' responsive question to heart and looked for answers. More than merely asking a question about bread and feeding people, Jesus seems to inquire of his disciples about their resources, their imagination in using those resources, and their openness to the power of God.

The Response of a Lead Follower

Jessi Langlie is Executive Director of Fletcher Place Ministries, which provides food, shelter, child care, and other services to some of the poorest of the population in the city of Indianapolis. As such, she is used to working with limited resources to meet people's needs. Here is her response:

Meeting the needs of our neighbors as we work to break the cycle of poverty on limited resources has been a challenge, but I wouldn't trade it for the world. When we have limited resources, we are forced to look more closely at the skills, energies, and passions we bring to the table. We are challenged by how we can creatively implement our gifts to achieve what needs to be done. Yes, funds are needed to keep the doors open, and there are sleepless nights trying to make that happen. Yet with limited resources we find that we may actually have an abundance of resources we would have ignored if we had plenty of money. Limited resources force us to use people resources, including people from local congregations and people in the area we serve. There is something that the homeless person can provide to help us meet our goals, and there is something that the single parent can offer that will help us move forward and be effective in our ministry. The formerly incarcerated bring something to the table, as well as the retired police officer. At the end of the day, it is about building relationships with a diverse group of people, something that might not have happened if we had an abundance of financial resources. We find the smile of God on each of our faces as we work together to meet the needs presented to us.

Reflect and Discuss

1. What resources are you overlooking in your efforts to follow Jesus?

2. What resources are being overlooked by your congregation?

3. Do you believe Jesus can work through people like us?

4. Do you believe that you can be an Andrew or an Andrea?

5. How do you balance being "realistic" with being "imaginative" in your efforts to be a Lead Follower?

Chapter Five

Lead Followers Leave behind their old Lives
(MARK 1:16-20)

Andrew left everything and followed Jesus. He was, in fact, one of the first four disciples whom Jesus called to follow him. He and his brother, Simon Peter, along with the brothers James and John, were invited to leave their nets, their business, and their families to come along on a journey of faith with Jesus of Nazareth. Their abandoned nets have become a symbol for leaving behind our old lives in order to follow a new life with Jesus.

Called to Be on a Team

When Jesus built a team of disciples, he began with two sets of brothers. Perhaps the four of them were already working together (it seems a likely possibility in the story). Even if not, being brothers would have given each pair a lifetime of practice working together, and the fact that they fished together required some teamwork. Fishing on the Sea of Galilee involved a cooperative effort of one person rowing the boat in circles while the other person carefully let down the folded nets into a large circle that would be drawn together to trap fish. That is why the request of the risen Christ to "cast your net on the right [other] side of the boat" (John 21:6) was such a strange instruction that yielded such unexpected results. It would be like asking someone to shift from doing a thing right-handed to doing it left-handed. Long-practiced teamwork would be difficult to change, but it is typical of Jesus to call his disciples (including us) to try a new pattern for better results.

Part of what Andrew and the other early disciples left behind was a sense of paramount individualism. Instead, Andrew was willing to become a part of a growing team of followers of Jesus. How have we in the church, at least in the West, moved so far toward individualism in our understanding of discipleship and ministry? Have we been so molded by the American culture into an individualist church with an individualistic gospel that we have lost sight of the call of Jesus to serve on a team in which we alternate between being leaders and followers?

As I supervise nearly 1,200 United Methodist congregations in the state of Indiana, I notice vast differences between churches that encourage teamwork and churches that do not. Many church staffs have developed a wonderful sense of "team," in which each person's gifts are honored, in which successes and achievements of staff members are celebrated together. I also have seen the reverse, in which the senior pastor treats the associate pastor and other staff members as flunkies who can't be trusted. Sometimes that has led to staff revolts or at least to staff dissension and lack of trust, and the whole congregation is hurt. And of course some staff persons cannot function well as team players, even when the senior pastor tries to set that style.

Likewise, it is apparent when a church functions around a good sense of "team" between clergy and laity and among the lay leadership. Such congregations usually thrive because all of the gifts of the body of Christ are being used and honored. As Paul's letter to the Corinthian church makes clear (1 Corinthians 12), followers of Jesus work best when they work as a team of different members all united for the good of the whole body.

I experienced the value of teamwork in my first church assignment as an associate pastor alongside a veteran senior pastor. Even though I was just out of seminary and quite inexperienced as a pastor, my senior pastor treated me like a real person and a real pastor. He insisted that the congregation refer to both of us as "pastors"—not as "senior" and "associate" pastors, and especially not as "senior" and "assistant" pastors as had happened previously with some staffs. The payoff for this collegial teamwork happened whenever anyone tried to pit us against each other. I remember a Sunday when I had preached, and a rather loud-voiced member of the congregation greeted me and said to the senior pastor, "You'd better watch out because this young man is a fine preacher." My senior pastor came over, put his arm around me, and quietly replied, "That's okay because we are on the same team." I learned a lesson that day about mutual respect, teamwork, and staying focused upon the good of the whole body.

Jesus began the process of teamwork with the calling of two sets of brothers to start building his team. His disciples did not always function as a team (as we will see later in part III), and neither do we in the current church. The lesson of Andrew and the other disciples is that whenever we allow self to become more important than team, we all suffer.

One of the inspiring coaches on the current scene in college basketball is Brad Stevens, the coach of the Butler University Bulldogs in Indianapolis. Brad is a member of the same congregation in which my wife serves on staff, and I have heard Brad share his understanding of the "Butler Way"—the values by which he recruits players and coaches his team. These values are captured in *Lead Like Butler: Six Principles for Values-Based Leaders* by Kent Millard (Nashville: Abingdon Press, 2012). In a time when individual players want to make the highlights on *SportsCenter* on ESPN, Brad's model is worth celebrating. He tells young athletes that coming to Butler means putting aside their own desires in order to help the team. The values of the Butler Way have become closely associated with the six principles of Butler basketball. The six principles as posted in the men's basketball locker room are as follows:

- Humility—know who we are, including strengths and weaknesses
- Passion—do not be lukewarm; commit to excellence
- Unity—do not divide our house; put the team first
- Servanthood—make teammates better; lead by giving
- Thankfulness—learn from every circumstance
- Accountability—no blaming; whenever anything goes wrong, ask the question: "What can I do to make it better?"

It would be wonderful if we in the church, especially those involved in the ministry of the clergy, would follow a similar pattern of teamwork. To do that, we need to leave behind our old life.

Leaving Behind Our Old Life

Andrew left behind more than just his fishing nets. He left behind his old life, and that is our challenge today. Our "old life" can include old habits that are unhealthy, old hurts that need to be healed, old dreams that are unfulfilled or unworthy, old prejudices that need to be challenged, old ideas that get in the way of faithful discipleship, and even our old identify as a self-made person. Jesus calls us to leave all of it behind in order to follow him and to be molded into Lead Followers.

Many persons have left behind lucrative careers to follow Jesus and be Lead Followers in his ministry, either as lay leaders or as clergy. One man served for twenty-five years as executive director of a chamber of commerce but left that lucrative position, sold his house, downsized his lifestyle, went through Local Pastors License School, and today serves with great joy and enthusiasm as a local pastor in a small but growing congregation. Not only did he make significant changes in his life, but also the witness of his changed life affected the many businesspeople with whom he used to work so closely. Many have come to him, sharing their own frustrations with the rat race of their lives, and he has helped them look for ways to find joy and hope by focusing upon spiritual issues.

I know a retired farming couple who heard the need for a ministry director on a reservation in the Dakotas. Using their ability to work hard and to fix just about anything, along with their down-to-earth approach to life, they moved to the reservation and became trustworthy members of the community in a place where the tribal leaders are often suspicious of Anglos who look like do-gooders. This couple simply lived their faith in an authentic way that made a difference in people's lives, with little fanfare, few funds, and lots of prayer. After leaving their old life behind, they were slowly accepted by the tribe, and countless lives have been affected by their faithfulness.

Many youth and young adults have made choices to leave behind an old life and to follow the calling and example of Christ. College students have given up the fun and sometimes-unhealthy activities of spring break to serve others on a mission trip. Countless youth at church camps have made a decision to follow Christ and have even considered the ministry as a vocation, even though such a choice could cause them ridicule back home with friends and classmates. Young adults who take the Christian faith seriously—expressing their doubts, exploring various faith expressions, and often becoming stronger disciples because of honest searches—always impress me.

There are changed lives in many ordinary congregations. People listen to the preaching, join small growth groups, perhaps serve in a hands-on ministry, and discover a new direction in their lives. Some of these stories are dramatic, but most involve subtle, small, and continuous changes from former lives and from a focus on self into a new life that is God-centered and other-focused. Those many changed lives are the real product of vital congregations all around the world.

Andrew Is Our Model

Andrew is our model, along with the other disciples and the larger group of followers of Jesus, which included women. Andrew is our paradigm of leaving behind an old life, risking change for the hope of the gospel, and finding a new life.

For Andrew, part of that risk and change was becoming known as "Simon Peter's brother." Even though Andrew started following Jesus before his brother, and even though Andrew played the key role in introducing his brother to Jesus (as we will see in the next chapter), Andrew was known as "the brother of" the more famous Simon Peter. Andrew apparently accepted that role, which this book is calling the role of Lead Follower, without severe objection. At least we do not have stories of Andrew quarreling with Simon Peter or the others about his importance. We don't have a story of Andrew and Simon making a special request for a preeminent position with Jesus (like we have with James and John). We don't even have any stories of Andrew criticizing Simon Peter for his denials of Jesus, for his lack of faith that made him sink like a rock when he tried to walk on water, or for his apparent inconsistencies. It is hard to imagine that two brothers like Andrew and Simon never argued, but the absence of such information in the Gospels leads us to assume that Andrew was able to take a secondary role without complaint. Perhaps Andrew followed Jesus by leaving behind not only his nets but also his own ego. As the next three chapters will demonstrate, Andrew is a model worth considering for our own efforts to leave behind our old life and to become a Lead Follower of Jesus.

An Inquiry from Jesus

"Simon, are you asleep? Couldn't you stay alert for one hour?" (Mark 14:37).

Jesus made this inquiry to Simon Peter, who slept while Jesus prayed in the Garden of Gethsemane. How difficult it must have been for Jesus to deal with disciples who were so human. Still today Jesus must wonder how his work can continue through people like us. Yet, Jesus called those first disciples, and Jesus calls us today. The inquiry is still relevant: are we asleep or awake to the call?

The Response of a Lead Follower

Craig LaSuer is Superintendent of the Northwest District of the Indiana Conference of The United Methodist Church, and his life story includes a time when he had to decide to leave behind his "old life" in order to follow Jesus. Here is his response:

I left behind a life of drugs. Due to various reasons, including dealing with a major chronic illness as I grew up, I turned to drugs to deal with the tough realities of life. This led to an addiction that lasted for quite a few years. But God never gave up on me, and in fact, God came looking for me! God sent many people to me as a part of my call to ministry, including God's own Spirit, and Jesus Christ himself. Jesus stood before me, offering a new life, but also asking me to leave behind the life of drugs that was destroying me. I said yes to his invitation. I told Jesus I'd make him my "main man" and never do drugs again. That was thirty-one years ago.

Jesus left behind certain ways to follow God's will and further God's kingdom all through his ministry even to the end as he died on the cross and then rose with everlasting resurrection power for all of humanity and the world.

The risen Christ stands before us now and says, "Leave behind what's trying to die, and embrace what's being born. Leave behind the plans you have, and follow my plan. Leave behind the dead ways of how your church does its business, and follow me into greater vitality and life-changing directions. Leave behind the messages of hopelessness and division that you hear in the world, and live out my message of unconditional love and kingdom power to all that you meet."

Reflect and Discuss

1. Another sermon by the Wesley brothers that prompted the Methodist revival was that of Charles Wesley, "Awake, Thou That Sleepest," which was preached at Oxford University on April 14, 1742. Where are you "asleep" as a disciple? Is your congregation awake or asleep to the call to discipleship?

2. If you have made the decision to follow Jesus, what have you left behind?

3. In what ways have you found your new life in Christ to be superior to your old life?

4. Where is Jesus still calling you to leave behind certain behaviors, ideas, addictions, hurts, or failures in order to be a better follower and leader?

5. In America we have had time periods called "great awakenings" of spiritual renewal. Is it possible that today is such a time?

Chapter Six

Lead Followers share the good news (John 1:40-42)

Andrew shared the news of Christ with his brother, Simon, even before Jesus called them to leave their nets and follow him. Andrew is historically important for bringing Simon to meet Jesus, and he is also a model of effective faith-sharing and evangelism. In contrast to some of the poor theology and ineffective practices called "evangelism" today, the Andrew model is biblical and effective.

It Started with John the Baptist

Andrew's quest for a new life of meaning and faithfulness to God began with following John the Baptist. John's message can easily sound like "bad news" today, but his coming was received by many of the people of his day as an indication of the dawning of God's activity and salvation in a terrible situation. John came in the midst of Roman occupation, characterized by oppressive taxes, incompetent governmental leaders, and corrupt religious leaders. Sounds like today, doesn't it? What we now call the first century A.D., or the first century of the Christian era, was a time of expectation and hope in the midst of despair. Times were bad for the people of Israel, and they longed for a Messiah to come and save them and to establish a new kingdom of God.

Into that highly charged situation, John appeared and called people to repentance. He was tough on the religious leaders of the day, but the common people flocked to him to be baptized as an act of repentance and preparation. John began to have followers, or disciples, and Andrew was among that group. Apparently some of the followers of John the Baptist continued to follow him even after Jesus appeared on the scene, but not Andrew. Andrew listened to the proclamation of John about Jesus when he said, "Look! The Lamb of God!" (John 1:36). Immediately Andrew and another follower of John began following Jesus.

Sharing Jesus with His Brother

Andrew wanted to share with his brother, Simon, the good news that he had found the promised Messiah. He invited Simon to come and meet Jesus. The encounter with Jesus began the transformation of Simon into Peter—a nickname that means "rock" or even "rocky." Jesus was already calling Simon to be more than he had been—to become a rock-solid Lead Follower.

Evidently it was later that Jesus walked along the Sea of Galilee and called Andrew and Simon to become official disciples, but it was Andrew's desire to share that led to this first meeting with Jesus.

A Model for Effective Evangelism

The "Andrew model" of faith-sharing and evangelism is contained within this story in the first chapter of the Gospel of John. It might be described this way:

- Spend time with Jesus because you can't share what you don't know.
- Share with your network of relationships: in this case, his brother, Simon.
- Share with "I" messages: Andrew said, "We [I] have found the Messiah" (John 1:41).
- Invite your friend/neighbor/colleague to meet Jesus.
- Leave the results up to Jesus because he is the one who saves and transforms.

This model, which seems simple and is easily taught, is in fact how Andrew shared his faith with his brother, who became the key leader of the disciples and the early church. One is left wondering: what if Andrew had not shared his experience and invited Simon to meet Jesus? Maybe Simon would have been drawn to Jesus on his own, maybe Jesus would have looked for Simon and invited him to be a disciple anyway, but maybe not. We will never know, but it is clear that Andrew played a key role in bringing Simon to Jesus.

The Hostility of Bad News Models

Followers of Jesus, especially Lead Followers, want to share the good news of that experience with others. There are many ineffective models that leave followers of Jesus feeling guilty or discouraged and that leave potential followers turned off. Indeed, some of those models seem not to deserve the name *evangelism,* which is about good news, because they come from a "bad news," or negative, approach.

I had a firsthand experience with a "bad news" approach. I had just moved to my first pastoral assignment after seminary, and I was busy unloading my rented truck. My wife and our baby were not yet with me, and the members of my church who helped me unload had gone home for the evening, so I was by myself, dressed in old clothes, working hard on a warm night. I heard a knock at the door and thought, "Oh good, another church member is here to help, or maybe a neighbor is here to welcome me to the neighborhood." Instead I discovered it was a man I had never met, dressed in black, who did not offer any greeting before demanding of me, "If you die tonight, do you know if you will go to heaven?" I answered yes and politely explained that I was the new Methodist pastor in town, which seemed to perplex him and take him off his prepared script. He muttered a few more words about his church offering salvation, and then he left. I went back to my unpacking, and a few minutes later I heard another knock at the door. He was back again, this time with a big smile, saying, "I also sell vacuum cleaners. Do you want to buy one?" Once again he disappeared as soon as I indicated that I already owned a vacuum cleaner. So much for that "evangelism" visit!

Even though I realize that experience was negative in the extreme, many of the least effective models of evangelism have this in common: they are based on *hostility* and not *hospitality.* I use the terms intentionally from a book by Henri Nouwen called *Reaching Out* (New York: Doubleday, 1975), in which he makes the point that many church people treat others with a hostility that is not necessarily violent but does not allow the "free and friendly space" of hospitality in which God can be at work. I believe Nouwen is correct, and I find that too much of what passes for evangelism is in fact thinly veiled hostility against those who do not yet accept our understanding of the Christian faith.

The Good News of the Andrew Model

The Andrew model is effective because it is based on simple biblical principles that are true to the good news of the gospel. First, it involves spending time with Jesus, being a follower oneself, growing in faith, and being ready to have a faith experience to share. Christian maturity helps us be ready to share our faith in a positive and helpful way. Second, the Andrew model asks us to share our faith across our natural human networks with those we already know and care about. Donald McGavran, in his classic book, calls these networks the "bridges of God." He brought home to the United States from the mission field the understanding that very few Christians are gifted in sharing their faith with strangers. However, all of us are called to witness to our faith with our friends, family, coworkers, and neighbors. The Andrew model calls us to use these bridges and networks. Third, the Andrew model involves sharing in "I messages" rather than the "you messages" of some other evangelism techniques. Rather than saying to his brother, Simon, "You need the Lord" or "Your life is a mess" or similar "you messages," Andrew shares an "I message" about his own encounter with Jesus. Such a witness has an integrity missing in "you messages." The Andrew model continues with inviting and bringing the other person to an opportunity to meet Jesus but then leaving the results up to Jesus. After all, we don't save anyone, we don't change anyone's life, and we don't transform anyone. Other models of evangelism perhaps operate with an arrogance that says, "I know you need the Lord, and I am here to fix you." The Andrew model avoids that approach and instead is an example of sharing the good news.

One of the oldest definitions of evangelism is often attributed to D. T. Niles: "one beggar telling another beggar where there is food to eat." The Andrew model is that kind of sharing of good news; it is one person telling another person, "Following Jesus has allowed the power of God to make a difference in my life." Such good news is easier to share than bad news, and it certainly is more effective.

By Invitation Only

Whatever model one uses for sharing the faith, it is clear that the gospel is shared by invitation only. Followers of Jesus are mandated to live as faithful witnesses to the power of the gospel. As one of my friends likes to put it, "We are not called to be salesmen, but we are called to be good examples of the merchandise." More than that, we are called to invite others to discover the joy, freedom, and power of following Jesus.

In the United States, Christians of all denominations and traditions don't do much sharing and inviting. Some statistics suggest that the average American Christian invites a friend to church once every thirty years! By contrast, in other places where the Christian movement is growing rapidly—such as South Korea, Africa, the Philippines, or South America—Christians tend to invite two other persons a week. Little wonder that their churches are growing.

How to invite and who to invite are questions that are answered by the

Andrew model. We are called to invite with "I messages" that share what God is doing in our lives, and we are called to share with those whom we already know and care about.

Andrew is a model of a Lead Follower who shows us how to share our faith effectively and faithfully in the name and style of Jesus.

An Inquiry from Jesus

"What are you looking for?" (John 1:38).

This was the question of Jesus to Andrew that caused Andrew to go and tell his brother that he had met Jesus. That question is one that needs to be answered by every person who wants to be a Lead Follower. What are we looking for in life? What kind of faith journey do we want? What do we want for our friends and loved ones?

The Response of a Lead Follower

Janie Reyes and her husband are copastors of the Iglesia Getsemani United Methodist Church in Fort Wayne, Indiana. Their growing Hispanic congregation is committed to sharing the good news of Jesus. Here is her response:

"What are you looking for?" is a question that I can answer these ways: I am looking to have an intimate relationship with Christ, to fall in love with him more and more every day, to know him more, to listen and obey him, and to be transformed each day by his presence. I look for more of Jesus every day in me. I look always to experience the great and awesome joy of sharing about Jesus, his transforming power, and his plan of salvation. I look for ways to share with all people how Jesus Christ transformed my life and took me out of darkness and into the light. And I am looking to invite people to know Jesus and lead them to him. I am always looking to plant in the hearts of the congregation a passion for Jesus and relationship with him that will create in them a passion to share Jesus with others.

I believe and teach this for myself and the congregation with whom God has entrusted me:

To live in a joyous and intimate relationship with Jesus that will cause us to feel the need for sharing Jesus.

To share our personal testimony with everybody—friends, relatives, and strangers—of how Jesus transformed our lives. We share every time we have an opportunity because we may very well be the last opportunity for that person to hear about Jesus and his plan of Salvation.

We invite them to receive Jesus.

We respect their decision.

I teach the church that we have been successful when we share and invite others to Jesus regardless of their decision; but if we do not share, that is not success.

Reflect and Discuss

1. Who in your life shared the faith with you in a powerful and persuasive way?

2. Did that person provide an authentic witness of a life lived as a follower of Jesus?

3. How and where did you first encounter Jesus as a real person and presence?

4. Who are the persons in your network of relationships to whom you can share about God's presence in your life in "I messages"? When will you find an opportunity to share, invite, and encourage those persons?

5. Are you ready to be an Andrew or Andrea for those persons?

Chapter Seven
Lead Followers Look for possibilities
(John 6:1-13)

Andrew was just an ordinary disciple. He was not often mentioned with Peter, James, and John. Perhaps he was a follower who stood more in the background, avoiding the limelight. And yet we find that Andrew was a follower who was always looking for possibilities.

Andrew Looked for Options

When the large crowd following Jesus needed to be fed, others said that Jesus should just send them away and get rid of the problem. Andrew was the one follower who looked for answers. He came to Jesus and said, to paraphrase, "There is this little kid with a sack lunch. It is not much, but maybe it is a start. And I trust that you, Jesus, can use this to help." What a great attitude! Instead of looking at the crowd of people as a problem, Andrew looked for possibilities. Instead of seeing obstacles, Andrew looked for opportunities. Instead of washing his hands of the issue, Andrew got his hands dirty looking for answers.

The answer that Andrew found was probably not much. Have you ever seen a little kid's sack lunch at the end of the day? It likely was sat upon, used to play catch with his friends, dropped into a mud puddle, or half-eaten. The other disciples might have dismissed it, saying, "There is no way it will feed the entire crowd." Not Andrew. Andrew did not have all of the answers, but Andrew was the kind of Lead Follower who looked for possibilities, even small ones. And Jesus was able to take the sack lunch and turn it into a way of feeding the whole crowd.

Bible scholars are divided in their explanations of how Jesus did that. Some say that he literally multiplied the sack lunch into overflowing baskets of food for everyone. Others say that Jesus took the small offering of the kid and of Andrew and used that as a motivation for everyone to share, and when everyone shared, everyone was fed. Either way, it was a miracle! And the miracle happened because one follower, Andrew, looked for possibilities and brought them to the attention of the leader.

Are You a Philip or an Andrew?

What kind of a follower are you? Are you like Andrew in the story, or are you perhaps like Philip? Philip is the one who says, "More than a half year's salary worth of food wouldn't be enough for each person to have even a little bit" (John 6:7). Philip looked at the enormousness of the problem, focused upon its impossibility, and refused to look further for answers. Are you like Philip in your family, in your church, and or in your work? Are you one who looks at what cannot be done?

Or are you a follower like Andrew? Are you one who, when faced with problems or obstacles, says, "There must be a way"? Do you offer helpful suggestions? Are you willing to risk offering an answer, even if it is only a small one? Are you often the avenue for others to find additional options?

It is easy to be a Philip (or a Phyllis) when confronted with problems or needs. It is easy to point out how difficult or impossible it is to find answers. It is easy to poke fun at the answers of others. It is easy to sit back, analyze the situation, proclaim, "It is impossible," and think that we are finished with an issue. Being an Andrew (or an Andrea) is a more difficult challenge. It requires hope, insight, risk-taking, and faith to follow Jesus and to be a Lead Follower.

Andrews (and Andreas) I Have Known

I have been blessed in my years of pastoral ministry by knowing several "Andrews" and "Andreas," who were the kind of Lead Followers who looked for possibilities. A family with a child who had special needs came to one church I served. Our Sunday school classes were not well prepared to handle the special needs of that child. Several people said in response, "Just tell that family we can't handle their child." But one woman in our church spoke up and said, "There must be many families in this area with special children. Maybe God is calling us to develop a whole new ministry for those families and their children." Her "Andrew" type of answer led us to develop a respite care program on Wednesday nights, whereby volunteers (and yes, she was the first one to volunteer!) received training and offered their services to care for children with special needs from 6:00 p.m. to 9:00 p.m. This program cared for the children and gave their parents a much-needed "respite" from the rigors of parenting children with special needs. Over the years, many new families were attracted to our church by this ministry. It all began with one woman who looked at the "problem" and saw possibilities.

In another situation, I served a church that discovered that it needed an expensive roof repair, costing nearly as much as their entire year's budget. Many were discouraged and even talked about closing the church. I was not sure how to lead the congregation through to a solution. But one older man in our church, a person who was a true "Andrew" follower, spoke up and said, "Since this problem is much too large for us to solve on our own, it is going to be fun to watch and see how God works through this situation." His positive perspective changed the whole tenor of our conversations, and we decided to trust God to fix the roof. Everyone gave, and many sacrificed; and when the bill came from the contractor, we paid it in cash from those extra gifts. Truly we had fun seeing how God worked through that situation, and it all started with one man who played the "Andrew" role in that moment.

While serving as Bishop in the Dakotas Area, I learned about one congregation that had tried for years to build a new church building. Everyone knew their old building was inadequate. Many talked about starting a building committee or perhaps a fund drive or even hiring an architect. But always the answer was the same: "We can't do it. It is too big a project. We don't have any money." Finally, one night in the midst of conversation about how "impossible" it would be to build a new church, one woman reached into her purse, took out $10, and said, "Here is the start of our building fund." Her donation was small, but her faith was large. Her gift got that church off dead center. They began giving to the fund, they worked on building plans, and after doing much of the construction themselves, they moved into their new facility. It all started with one woman—an "Andrea"—who offered what she had and inspired everyone to help solve the issue.

Do You Know an Andrew or an Andrea?

Surely there are such stories in your life and in your church. Surely there are people who have been an "Andrew" or an "Andrea" for you. Remember, though, that like Andrew in the Gospels, such persons are often quiet, self-effacing, and working hard in the background. Sometimes they are overlooked, but always they are strategic to the other followers of Jesus and to his mission. Perhaps you have been an "Andrew" or "Andrea" yourself, helping find answers, offering solutions, and looking for possibilities. One of the spiritual dimensions of Christian leadership and followership is the ability, the willingness, and the faith to look for possibilities. It is one of the important ways that we can be Lead Followers.

Do You Believe God Is Already Doing Miracles Today?

Several years ago I led a Bible study in my church, and we studied the miracles of Jesus—how he fed people, healed people, and so on. In the midst of the study, a young woman who was new to our church and new to the Christian faith asked me an interesting question. She said, "Do you believe God is still doing miracles today?" Before I could answer, an older woman who was a longtime Christian and member of our church, but who usually was rather quiet, surprised all of us by answering quite loudly, "No! You are asking the wrong question. I don't believe God is still doing miracles today. I believe God is already doing miracles today, and we haven't seen anything yet!"

Her answer was better than any answer I might have given, and she expressed her own faith very well. What do we believe? Do we believe the Bible is a story of what God used to do, and maybe if we pray really hard then God might have one small miracle left for us before God runs out of gas? Or do we believe the Bible is a record of what God already has been doing, in order for us to learn to see God's miracles every day in our lives? Which way is it? To be a Lead Follower after the model of Andrew is to look for the miracles God is already doing.

An Inquiry from Jesus

"Do you believe I can do this?" (Matt. 9:28).

Jesus asked this question to two blind men before he healed them. Jesus understood that not even those who asked him for help were certain that he could help them. His question helps sort out the "Andrew" followers from the "Philip" followers. How about us? Do we believe Jesus can do this? If so, then we will look for possibilities like Andrew did. If not, then we will respond like Philip and dismiss possibilities.

The Response of a Lead Follower

Kayc Mykrantz is the co–lay leader of the Indiana Conference and a staff person with the Crosswind United Methodist Church in Logansport, Indiana. In both roles she finds answers to situations and entrusts them to Jesus. Here is her response:

Working on a church staff, I observed the way my pastor crafted funeral messages. He would call the family together, and they would discuss poignant memories of their loved one, the qualities that made him or her unique, and his or her favorite Bible verses and stories of faith. He would weave those things together in a way that not only ministered to the family but also was a tribute to the person who had passed.

When my own mother died, our family members met with her pastor. We, too, spilled out precious memories and tears. Unfortunately, however, although we had discussed many issues of faith, Mother had never shared her favorite Bible verses with any of us. I despaired when, after a thorough search of her home, I could not find her Bible. In grief and disappointment, I prayed. Then I found a passage and shared it with her pastor. As he shared with those of us gathered at the funeral, I thanked God for his help in choosing verses that described her so perfectly. It was a wonderful celebration of her life.

A year later, Dad found and sent Mother's Bible to me. I was dumbfounded when I leafed through the pages and found that the only passage marked and dated was the exact Scripture God had given me!

It is those "miraculous" experiences in our lives that fan our faith to bright flame. Whatever we give him, whether fishes and loaves, or a desperate cry for help, God responds with the right answer and with love everlasting.

That lesson helped me when I was a part of the group that first worked to bring together our two conferences in Indiana. We talked and talked and talked some more. We were good thinkers. We loved the church. We loved the people in the more than 1,200 congregations that would make up the new conference. We each brought to the table a list of the bountiful gifts and talents that already existed in our respective individual conferences. However, we had no idea how to begin to do the work we knew would be necessary for that vitally important first step.

"Let's ask God."

I don't remember which of us had that novel idea, but the five of us bowed our heads and prayed. The prayer flowed with the kind of vulnerability we had been unable to develop in our conversation, no matter how hard we had tried. And then our prayer moved to a new place, a place where God not only hears but also responds by adding his own voice. It was at that point that we were inspired to consider not a merger but creating something new. By the time we left that room, we were no longer five individuals with an impossible task. We were a team of five plus the One who would walk with and lead us and others through a years-long journey of creating together.

When we give God what we have, in faith, and invite him to be who he is among us, he gives us the inspiration, strength, and ability to leap over walls. Though we might not be able to accomplish much on our own, by giving him our little, the Great Multiplier makes more than we could ask or imagine. We were able to, as we named the new creation, "Imagine Indiana."

Reflect and Discuss

1. Have you ever offered what you believed was a good idea, only to have someone be a "Philip" and dismiss it?

2. Have you known people who are an "Andrew" or an "Andrea" in their ability to look for possibilities? Do you find such persons to be inspiring?

3. When have you been an "Andrew" or "Andrea" and found a possibility that bore fruit?

4. As you seek to lead, do you look for "Andrews" or "Andreas" who can help you find new possibilities? Have you found such persons to be a part of your leadership team?

5. Do you believe that Jesus can take your seemingly small offerings and do something amazing and miraculous?

Chapter Eight

Lead Followers break down barriers (John 12:20-26)

Philip began to understand that Andrew was a Lead Follower. When some Greeks came to Philip, who may have been Greek in heritage, and wanted to see Jesus, Philip at least understood that Andrew might be the one who could help with their request. We are not sure who these Greeks were, but typically such persons were regarded as foreigners and outsiders who could not cross cultural barriers to approach Jesus. So Philip told Andrew, who then told Jesus. Even though the response of Jesus was not easy to hear, because Jesus warned them about the demands of discipleship, at least Philip and Andrew overcame some of the typical barriers of the first century and took the risk of bringing these outsiders to Jesus.

Barriers in Jesus' Day

Society during Jesus' time was full of barriers that kept people apart. Of course, the general population was held under the dominance of their Roman occupation, so only a few local leaders who cooperated with Roman authorities were accepted into governmental leadership positions. Everyone else was outside of the political barrier.

Barriers existed between those who tried to live within the constraints of the Roman occupation and those, such as the Pharisees—the "separated ones"—who tried to live by a rigid set of religious rules, especially dietary and cleanliness rules, which kept them separated from both the Roman authorities and from ordinary people. Another huge barrier existed between Jews of the Judean and Galilean provinces and half-breed Jews who lived in the province of Samaria and had intermarried with non-Jews. The Jewish/Samaritan barrier is reflected in many of the teachings of Jesus, including his shocking story of the good Samaritan who treats a wounded man like a neighbor (Luke 10:25-37).

Another major barrier existed between men and women, with some

Jewish leaders urging men not to have contact or conversation with women outside their own families. Jesus' dialogue with the Samaritan woman at the well in the fourth chapter of the Gospel of John is an amazing demonstration of the willingness of Jesus to cross not one, but two significant barriers: Samaritans and women.

Perhaps the largest barrier of Jesus' day was the one between Jews and Gentiles. Some of the teachings of the Jewish rabbis of Jesus' day reflect the distrust, prejudice, and downright hatred of such nonbelievers. We see in chapter fifteen of the book of Acts how the early church struggled in dealing with Gentiles who had become followers of Jesus. It is fortunate and largely a testament to the power of the Spirit that early church leaders decided to overcome the Jew/Gentile barrier and thus allow the gospel to spread even further.

Barriers in Our Day

Before we dismiss first-century Jewish culture as a time of many barriers, we need to acknowledge the barriers of our own time and place. Some modern-day barriers are the obvious ones: race, gender, age, wealth, sexual orientation, and politics. Many of these barriers affect us in the church, as well as theological barriers that we often characterize as liberal and conservative.

However, perhaps the most subtle and difficult barrier congregations face is the difference between "preference" and "purpose." Chapter 1 noted how our possessions can lead us to value our own preferences over the purpose or mission of being a follower of Jesus. A barrier divides these two totally different perspectives of reality, and it becomes an often-unspoken or unrecognized basis for nearly every decision, dissension, and dialogue in the life of every congregation.

The barrier between preference and purpose often causes conflict and even schism within congregations as they make decisions about budget, building use, programs, ministries, and, of course, priorities. One congregation with which I am familiar faced this barrier when they suddenly received a large inheritance that came unexpectedly from a former member who had moved away many years earlier. The congregation was faced with making decisions about how to use their windfall. Those on the "preference" side of the barrier wanted to use the funds to remodel their old building or to endow the costs of ongoing maintenance of the building or to invest the money and use the interest income to reduce the demands of their annual budget. On the other side of the congregational divide were those who believed such funds should go to the "purpose" of the church—perhaps hiring more staff to lead outreach ministries or immediately giving 10 percent or more to various mission projects or even giving all of the money away "so that it will not negatively impact our stewardship." Given the separate lists of choices, anyone can see how the often-ignored barrier of preference/purpose reared itself within that congregation for many months!

Andrew Overcame a Barrier

In the story of the Greeks, Andrew apparently was perceived, at least by Philip, as one who would overlook or overcome barriers and bring people to Jesus who did not "fit" into the expected categories of his other followers and disciples. We wish we knew more of this story: Who were these Greeks? Were they Jews who lived within Greek culture? Were they possibly even Gentiles? Were they just curiosity-seekers who had heard about Jesus and wanted to see a celebrity? Or were they persons who were genuine candidates for becoming his followers?

The response of Jesus would seem to indicate that he took them seriously, and thus he warned them how difficult it is to be a disciple. Jesus was in fact drawing closer to his own sacrifice, so he offered them the image of a seed that must die in order to provide life. He compared discipleship to being willing to die or at least to following Jesus to his own death. If these Greeks were just curiosity-seekers, why would Jesus offer such a tough description of discipleship? It seems more likely that Jesus saw their genuine desire to be followers and he responded accordingly.

No matter how we understand the request of the Greeks, Andrew is once again a Lead Follower who overcame barriers of his day to help others become followers of Jesus. Philip's respect for Andrew's leadership is also obvious in this passage, for by now Andrew has emerged as a follower of Jesus who is also a leader: a Lead Follower. Andrew's reputation as a Lead Follower is enhanced by his willingness to cross some of the same barriers that Jesus himself crossed so easily.

How Do We Overcome Barriers?

Overcoming barriers was not easy in Jesus' day, and it is not any easier in our day. Once we become genuine followers of Jesus who believe that such barriers are not only inappropriate but also contrary to the emerging kingdom of God, how do we overcome such barriers?

Many common strategies for overcoming barriers seem to be ineffective. Some believe, for example, that it is just a matter of education: "Let's just help people learn about their differences, and then they will no longer allow those differences to divide them." Certainly it is true that some barriers and prejudices and differences in our contemporary culture are the result of ignorance and lack of exposure to people who are different. However, given the access to media, the availability of Internet resources, and the mobility of people, it is hard to imagine that simply more education or awareness of others will remove the many barriers that divide people in our time. We already have much information about others, yet our information does not seem to reduce prejudices and barriers. Perhaps deeper education could help, but how does anyone impose such education on the broad spectrum of people?

Another strategy is to "overlook our differences" and just treat everyone the same. Some seem to suggest that we would be better off ignoring the cultural, ethnic, and political differences that divide us: "Let's just treat everyone the same." Usually this strategy is taken by persons in the majority culture, and their approach is akin to the old "melting pot" ideal that suggests minority-culture persons lose their uniqueness and join the majority culture. Of course, the problem with that strategy is, who wants to be in someone else's melting pot? For the various minority cultures, losing their uniqueness into the majority culture is not very attractive.

Another strategy for overcoming barriers today is the idea of "diversity training" so that we can learn to appreciate differing experiences and thus value our diversity. Certainly such training is helpful for everyone to learn new ways of relating to one another, but this strategy often fails because those who most need such training are the least likely to receive it. Even when we made diversity training a requirement for the clergy of our Indiana Conference, for example, we had to deal with those who did not attend or who attended reluctantly because, in their view, they "did not need to learn about that," because they did not perceive themselves as having a problem.

A Better Way

Jesus offers a better way, a more complete transformation, and an eternal answer to the barriers that divide us. He invites us to die in order to live. He invites us to give in order to receive. He invites us to love in order to stop hating.

That was Jesus' answer to the visiting Greeks whom Andrew brought to him. Jesus apparently accepted and welcomed them, and he responded to their desire to see him and perhaps to follow him, but he did so by pointing to a higher calling. The calling he described was the very one he was accepting: the call to love deeply enough to die. He talked of seeds falling into the ground and dying in order to live. He warned the Greeks, his other disciples, and us today that following him is not easy.

Jesus teaches us that risking love actually brings us life, even if through death. We have so many examples of persons who have reinforced that teaching: Martin Luther King, Jr., and Mother Teresa come to mind quickly. So, too, do the names of countless persons who are not famous or celebrities, but who quietly give themselves away for others and whose lives testify to the life-giving characteristics that lead to life-receiving results.

You Only Have to Die

The Reverend James Harnish, the pastor of Hyde Park United Methodist Church in Tampa, Florida, has authored a wonderful book titled *You Only Have to Die* (Nashville: Abingdon Press, 2004). His book tells the story of his own near-death experience and how he was prompted to lead his congregation to overcome the barriers of the past, their own mental images, and the divide between preference and purpose—and thus to "die" to their old way of being a church to find life in new forms and efforts.

Harnish makes a point worth consideration by all Christians and especially by all Christian leaders who want to be a Lead Follower of Jesus. By relating the story of his life-changing illness, he shares how he was freed to be able to "die" to his older ideas and concepts and practices of ministry in order to find new life. In addition, his story tells of helping his congregation overcome a variety of barriers in order to find new life. Together the two stories illustrate the message of Jesus: being a disciple who overcomes barriers is a journey that involves death in order to find life.

Want to overcome the barriers that divide us today? You only have to die. That answer sounds harsh and shocking. Can't we just all get along? Can't we just overlook our differences? Can't we just treat everyone the same? Can't we just give everyone diversity training? The answer of Jesus is, "No, you have to die in order to overcome the barriers that keep us apart and the barriers that keep us from God." Only by dying to ourselves do we find life in Christ and tear down the barriers that divide us from one another.

Everyone Is a Candidate for Resurrection

One of my favorite memories from my years as a pastor was an expression of an older, longtime member of the congregation. His name was Ed, and he was a retired owner of a small grocery store—the kind of neighborhood grocery store that seems to have faded from our U.S. culture. Ed loved people. Even though he was Anglo and from a poorer background, often characterized as a "redneck," Ed was a gracious person who served as a kind of "permanent greeter" at our church for Sunday services and all other events. Even though other persons might have been assigned as the official greeters for a service or event, Ed was always on hand, always greeting new people, always making folks feel welcome.

One time when we were eating lunch in a local restaurant after Ed had served as a volunteer in our church office that morning (yes, he was always around the church, helping others), I asked Ed how he was able to be so open and hospitable to all persons. His answer startled me, but I have remembered it over the years. He said, "Well, I look at any person I see as a candidate for resurrection." To my blank expression, he further explained, "Jesus died for everyone, didn't he? Everyone is invited to new life in Christ, aren't they? That's why everyone is a candidate for resurrection."

Looking back, I realize how much Ed was a Lead Follower in our church. Ed died several years ago, but I sense that he is still overcoming barriers, inviting everyone to the resurrection banquet, and giving that knowing smile that says, "See, I knew you were a candidate for resurrection."

Andrew: Our Paradigm of a Lead Follower

Andrew was a Lead Follower of Jesus who seems to have understood the lessons of Jesus—lessons that were spoken, demonstrated, and lived. Andrew began following Jesus as soon as John the Baptist pointed to Jesus and declared him to be "the Lamb of God." Andrew found in Jesus the One who could show him the way, even if that way was the way of the cross.

Andrew was also a leader, even if his leadership style was subtler than the style of his brother, Simon. Andrew always seemed to find options, to look for possibilities, to share his faith experience, and to overcome barriers. Andrew was often listed as simply "the brother of Simon Peter," and yet Andrew was a Lead Follower in his own right. His model is inspiring, encouraging, and illustrative of a style of leadership that is desperately needed in the church today. In part III we will look more deeply into the implications of this Lead Follower model, and we will consider how all of us are invited to become better leaders by becoming better followers of Jesus.

An Inquiry from Jesus

"What do you think about the Christ? Whose son is he?" (Matt. 22:42).

Jesus asked this question of some Pharisees who needed to overcome their own mental barriers. They often debated with Jesus because they took seriously their Hebrew Scriptures, but they also seemed to get "stuck" in minor details. In this case they simply could not understand how the Christ could be someone like Jesus—someone who was always overcoming barriers that the Pharisees believed had been erected by the Hebrew Scriptures and the religious teachings of the day. Jesus' inquiry reminds us that the largest barriers we face to following him are our own mental constructs and understandings. Just when we think we have God figured out, our categories and understandings are challenged by the gospel.

The Response of a Lead Follower

Charles Harrison is the pastor of Barnes United Methodist Church in Indianapolis, the largest African American UM congregation in Indiana. He has led that congregation to stay in a tough neighborhood to make a difference by helping people overcome their own personal barriers. Here is his response:

> There are several barriers I face daily in my life and ministry as I seek to do God's will. I struggle sometimes in overcoming my sense of failure, when I am not sure the work for Christ I am doing in the congregation and the community is really making a difference in people's lives. I struggle also with not allowing my own expectation of what I want to see happen as a disciple of Christ to become a barrier to what God is trying to accomplish through me.
>
> The goal of Barnes United Methodist Church is to become a transformational presence in the community we serve. What holds the Barnes congregation back from having a more effective ministry in our neighborhood is the fear that we lack the resource to truly meet the needs of the people in the communities we serve.
>
> In my office I have a picture of President Barack Obama, who overcame many barriers to become the first black president of America. Candidate Barack Obama was able to break down the barrier of racism to accomplish God's purpose for him. As a follower of Jesus Christ, I have no barriers in my life and ministry that I cannot

overcome. The cross reminds me of God's call on my life and how, like Jesus, I am called to give myself away for the sake of Christ. When we are able to give as Christ gave to us, then we can give ourselves away to others, and we can break down the barriers and differences to lead others to a complete transformation in Christ.

Reflect and Discuss

1. What barriers do you most often encounter in your life and ministry?

2. What barriers are holding your congregation back from more effective ministry?

3. In addition to some of the noteworthy examples of those who have overcome barriers listed in this chapter (Martin Luther King, Jr., and Mother Teresa), who are other noteworthy persons who have broken down barriers? Was their method similar to the teaching of Jesus about a seed falling into the soil and dying in order to bring forth life?

4. When you consider following Jesus all the way to the cross, what does the image of the "cross" mean in your life and ministry? Are you willing to die in order to live? To give in order to receive? To love in order to overcome hatred?

5. Are you willing to be a Lead Follower of Jesus?

PART III
the qualities of a Lead Follower

We have considered those who were "almost followers" but were unable to follow Jesus and Andrew as a paradigm of a follower and a leader (what we are calling a *Lead Follower*), and the next four chapters examine the qualities of a Lead Follower.

As we read about Jesus in the Gospels, we also read about his disciples. We discover that they too often fell into the trap of competition rather than seeing discipleship as a "dance" of being a leader and a follower (this book calls that "dance" being a Lead Follower). The disciples seemed often to misunderstand Jesus, to be clueless to the meaning of his parables, and, even worse, to fail him when he most needed a supportive team. Yet Jesus kept working with them, helping them become followers who would become the leaders of his movement and his church after his own death.

Seeing Jesus be patient with the disciples in the Gospels gives us hope that Jesus is patient with us. We fail him often, and we too often become competitors rather than cooperative members of the Jesus team. In our own subtle ways, even in our efforts to be a great leader for a good cause, we too often fall into the trap of being the kind of leader who is unable to follow Christ or other Christian leaders.

The very fact that the church today continually cries out for leadership is an indication of the lack of teamwork and cooperation among the followers of Jesus. If we were better followers of Jesus—persons who did a better job of imitating the style and person of Jesus—we might discover that leadership is a shared experience, an ongoing "dance" between being a leader and a follower, and a product of the community of faith. That we in the church look for someone to be a leader who will save us is an indication that we are not following the One who is already the Savior.

An Inquiry from Jesus

"What were you arguing about during the journey?" (Mark 9:33).

Jesus addressed the disciples who debated one another about who was the greatest. Once again we see the disciples of Jesus not understanding this team to which Jesus had called them. Just as we saw the brothers James and

John jockey for positions of privilege, we see in this inquiry how Jesus challenged their misunderstanding that leadership is about privilege rather than servanthood.

Can you picture the scene? Likely the disciples were following Jesus down some dusty road or path in a meandering line. Even as they followed the One who kept refusing to allow the people to crown him a king (John 6:14-15), these same disciples argued about their own greatness and privilege. Even as they followed the One who said that they should not "show off their authority" like the Gentiles (Mark 10:42), these same disciples tried to exercise their own authority over one another. Even as they followed the One who was on his way to the cross to give himself for others, these same disciples tried to grab and take positions of leadership.

The Response of a Lead Follower

Jenifer Stuelpe-Gibbs serves on the staff of First United Methodist Church in Bloomington, Indiana, where she has been a strong leader/follower during a time of staff transition. Here is her response:

> Jesus waited to question his disciples until they were in the house and quiet enough to really listen to him. Those who mouthed off about their greatness moments before responded with silence. Whether the silence was born of guilt or reverence is of no consequence. That response, and nothing more, was their moment of greatness. I am learning the value of that silence.
>
> I serve a multistaff-member church in transition. In four years, eleven staff changes have occurred. In the midst of change it can be easy to blame one another, which is the crux of the problem. When I find myself contending with jealous, territorial, or unsuccessful feelings, it is because I stop contending with the mission of following Jesus and start comparing. The argument about greatness is not only about privilege but also about fear. The quiet fear of not measuring up often yields the loudest arguments.
>
> After their argument, Jesus asks the question, and it echoes in their silence. The silence is the space in which they turn back to him. Leaders become followers again, and they stand shoulder to shoulder as teammates and not as contenders. Our greatness becomes about yielding to the One who called us to lead and teaches us to serve. We

are not left to respond only with silence, however. Just a few chapters later, Jesus defines greatness by a widow who holds out her one mite as an offering. As I learn to lead by first sitting in silence with Christ, I think of her often. I remember that we all bring our one mite to offer.

Reflect and Discuss

1. Have you ever felt jealous of another follower of Jesus who seemed to have superior leadership qualities?

2. Have you ever been pushed aside by another Christian who wanted to take the lead on some project, some worship service, or some ministry?

3. When you hear about the success of another pastor or another congregation, do you feel jealous? Do you feel unsuccessful just because of their success?

4. Are you tired of waiting to be rewarded for being a faithful follower of Jesus?

5. Do you think of leadership as a privilege to be received or as a service to be offered?

Chapter Nine

Lead Followers Are Loyal to their Leader
(John 6:66-68)

Loyalty is a lost commodity in today's world. Businesses are not loyal to their employees, and employees are not loyal to their employers. My father graduated from Purdue University in 1947, after having his college education disrupted by serving in World War II. He went to work for General Motors, worked there in various capacities for forty years, and then retired. Such loyalty to one company and such loyalty to an employee was commonplace during Dad's career. When was the last time you heard a recent example of such loyalty?

Loyalty is not even prevalent in families today. Husbands and wives are not loyal to each other; children and parents are not loyal. We all know about the divorce rates, and no families are unaffected. Most schools and most Sunday schools have to deal with the joint-custody issues of the children they are trying to teach. Even when an actual divorce does not happen, many marriages are not based upon loyalty. How many married persons engage in online flirtations with other persons?

Even in church, people are not loyal to their denomination. So when they move to a new community, they do not necessarily look first for a new congregation with the same denominational "brand." Many people are not even loyal to their own local congregation if the "next pastor" does not measure up to the current one. Perhaps most alarming, too many Christians are not even loyal to Christ.

Lead Followers Are Loyal

Lead Followers are loyal. Their loyalty is not a "blind loyalty" but an "open-eyed loyalty," which understands costs and implications. Jesus cannot be accused of making discipleship seem easy or of oversimplifying the challenge of following him. No, Jesus makes it clear that he wants his followers to know the cost, the price, and the danger; but he does want loyalty. He even says that "no one who...looks back" can be a part of the kingdom of God (Luke 9:62).

To be a follower of Jesus—especially a follower of Jesus who also is a leader of other Christians—requires loyalty. Such loyalty does not always mean total agreement or uniformity or unanimity, but it does mean faithfulness to one another and to Christ.

The Loyal Opposition

A few years ago I was consecrating a building addition for a church that had worked and struggled to accomplish their task. With their new construction and remodeling finally finished, they gathered to celebrate that effort. I knew from some correspondence I had received from various members that this had not been a unanimous effort. Several people in that congregation had voted no and had expressed their doubts about the project. So I was curious to see how the day of their celebration would be handled.

I was pleasantly surprised by the tone, attitude, and words of the layperson who had chaired their building project. In the midst of thanking lots of people who had dreamed of, given to, worked on (several in their congregation had literally worked on the construction), and supported the project, he added these words: "And now, I want to express my appreciation to those of you who were a part of the loyal opposition. Some of you were not in favor of this project, and you asked tough questions all along the way. Those questions helped us sharpen and streamline our project, and those ongoing concerns caused us to rethink at several points. But you remained loyal to this church throughout the project, and many of you worked hard to put up drywall and paint. You of the loyal opposition deserve a special word of appreciation." Rousing applause from everyone present followed his amazing statement.

Such "loyal opposition" is a wonderful thing to see, and it is a model that we in the church should be able to offer to society at large. In a time of political and social polarization, we in the church who follow Jesus should be able to offer an alternative way of getting along: the concept of loyal opposition. The term *loyal opposition* has most often been used in the British government as a label for the party that is not in power, but sadly even in Britain this concept seems to be waning. We in the church, who are followers of Jesus, should be able to do better. We can disagree with one another, but we can remain in the loyal opposition.

My Personal Hero

When I was growing up in my home church, the lay leader of the congregation, Roy, was a kind of hero for me. He was certainly a leader, and his leadership was noticed by others. He was elected six times as a lay delegate to the General Conference of the Methodist Church. He was a perennial lay member of the annual conference. He was a leader in every sense of the word, but that is not why he was my hero.

Roy was my hero for two reasons. One was his passion for the ministry of the church. When our church building burned on the Saturday night before Christmas when I was in the sixth grade, Roy and the pastors of our church put together a hastily organized worship service at the local high-school auditorium. Roy was the one who first sounded the theme of that day and of the next several years: "Our church did not burn. Our building burned, but the church is the people, and the people will go on." Over and over again during the next several years, Roy was the right leader for the right time for that congregation. Rebuilding proved to be difficult; and for several years, we were a large congregation without a building. We met for worship in the high-school auditorium and later in the local movie theatre. We had Sunday school classes at the YMCA and in local coffee shops. We rebuilt, but it took a lot of faith and loyalty for people to stay with that long process. Roy led the way with his constant statement: "Our church did not burn. Our building burned, but the church is the people, and the people will go on."

The second reason Roy became my hero was the way he handled being outvoted. During the long decision process about rebuilding, many people, including Roy, believed that it was a good time to relocate to a larger property and to leave the old site downtown. Hot debate followed, and even as a kid I was aware of the disagreements. Finally there was a congregational meeting to vote on the subject, and Roy made one of his usual impassioned speeches. When the vote was taken, his position was not supported. To my surprise, Roy was immediately on his feet, asking to speak again. He was reluctantly recognized by the district superintendent, who may have feared the worst. But Roy said these words, or something very close to these words, that I remember so well: "The church has spoken. The decision has been made. Now it is up to all of us to get behind this decision and make it work."

I was in awe that such a strong, passionate leader could also be so humble and cooperative and supportive of a decision he had opposed. Roy became an even bigger hero to me that day, and his model of loyalty still inspires me. Roy was truly a Lead Follower.

Lead Followers Are Loyal When They Are Not Leading

The lesson I learned from Roy (and from other persons who have been a part of the loyal opposition) is simply this: Lead Followers are loyal even when they are not leading. It is easy to be loyal when all of the decisions are going my way. It is easy to be loyal when I am leading and others are following. And it is easy to be loyal when I am following a leader who is doing things that I support. The real challenge for Lead Followers is whether we will allow others to lead and whether we will be loyal to Christ and the church even when our own leadership is not being approved.

The Key Characteristics of Loyalty

Consider these key characteristics of loyalty. Hopefully these characteristics are obvious in the previous stories and in the gospel narrative, but it helps to make plain such a list:

- Loyalty is not based upon personality, but on the mission of the group.
- Loyalty is consistent, not unreliable.
- Loyalty is creative, but not impulsive.
- Loyalty is trustworthy, never dishonest.
- Loyalty is faithful, even when others are disloyal.

Such a list of the characteristics of loyalty is always incomplete; loyalty is something that is hard to define but obvious when it is observed.

Loyalty and Perspective

I have lived in several university towns and have watched the ebb and flow of the loyalty of the sports fans of those universities. In particular I have noticed how some fans seem only to be loyal when the team is doing well. In one situation a coach came to a university with great fanfare, with many in the media mentioning him with all-time great coaches before he had coached even one game at the school. True to form, his team began to win and to win big in the early season over what some sportswriters called the "cupcake" teams on its schedule. The loyal fans were in a near frenzy. Then came the more difficult parts of the schedule, and the team began to lose some games.

They finished with a winning record for the year but disappointed some pre-season forecasts.

Most of the fans maintained their loyalty, with lots of articles and comments about how "this was just the first year" for the new coach. Many still forecast great days ahead, perhaps an undefeated season, and certainly multiple national championships. The second and third seasons were not much improved; the team still had winning records, but just barely. Year four was a disaster as the team fell into a losing season and the calls of "loyal fans" for the firing of the coach became nearly impossible to ignore. To their credit, university leaders issued a statement, saying, "We gave the new coach a five-year contract, and so he will be our coach next year, after which we will evaluate whether or not to renew his contract." Fans went crazy, especially accusing the university of being disloyal to the fans.

Sadly, the fifth year was not an improvement, and the coach's contract was not renewed. Many people applauded the loyalty and integrity of the university. They had given the coach a five-year contract and had stuck to it. They stood by him when it would have been easy to appease the crowds and fire him.

I watched the whole situation, and I believe the loyalty of the university was based on a longer-term perspective. What if they had reneged on their contract and fired him sooner? What kind of coach would have been willing to come to that university in the future? What does the long-term perspective have to say about sports and education? What perspective offers the most integrity?

Lead Followers are not just loyal in the short term; they have a long-term perspective on loyalty. Skilled leaders who are also followers of Jesus know that they don't have to "win" every decision, and they know that short-term setbacks are not the end of the story. Loyalty is best when it has the perspective of time, maturity, wisdom, and persistence.

Loyalty Requires Persistence

American Express was loyal to me. Many years ago I had an American Express card, but I eventually gave it up when I began using other cards. That is when I began to learn about the persistence of American Express and its desire to keep me as a loyal customer. First, they called me, more than once, to ask me very politely why I had cancelled my American Express card. Rather than try to convince me that I was wrong, their callers were very hospitable, gracious, and pleasant on the phone. They seemed truly to want to understand, as they put it, "where we have let you down." So I explained about their fees being higher than those of other cards, their limited areas of service (in those days), and my decision to switch to another type of credit card. They seemed to be noting my responses, asking only information-seeking questions, not blaming questions, and they responded without animosity or hurt. They were, in fact, responding the way I would hope a good friend might respond to a broken friendship. Still, I had decided to switch cards, and they accepted that fact.

To my surprise, American Express called me nearly fifteen years later. I had moved three times since those previous phone conversations, and in fact I was now living in Fargo, North Dakota. I have no idea how they found me, but they called to say that they had a new product that might interest me because it fit the criteria I had named all of those years before when I cancelled their card. I was nearly speechless to think that a credit card company was that persistent in its efforts to be loyal to me and to keep me as a customer. Of course, the company wanted my business, but its approach was one of hospitable persistence, not a pushy effort to "sell" me. Most important, it seemed that their callers had truly listened to me, something we will consider in chapter 10.

American Express was loyal to me, and I finished that conversation wondering how many local congregations would listen to their former members who had left them for another church, keep such a record of their concerns, and then respond years later with new ministry opportunities to meet the needs of those former members. I can't imagine any local congregation being that loyal, can you?

Loyalty requires persistence: the kind of persistence that lasts over years, that listens and remembers concerns, that responds with new possibilities, and that never gives up.

Lead Followers Are Loyal

It bears repeating: Lead Followers are loyal, even when they are not leading and even when the team or the congregation or the group is not agreeing with the Lead Follower. Lead Followers are loyal, and they never give up being a follower of Jesus.

An Inquiry from Jesus

"Do you also want to leave?" (John 6:67).

At a time when many of the crowds who had followed Jesus were starting to leave and fade away, Jesus asked the twelve disciples this haunting inquiry.

Simon gave the response we all hope we would give: "Lord, where would we go? You have the words of eternal life. We believe and know that you are God's holy one" (John 6:68-69). Although it is clear in so many places in the Gospels that Simon Peter did not fully understand Jesus, and while we know that Simon Peter would three times deny he even knew Jesus, still his answer at this moment is a valuable response of loyalty. Simon responded as we all want to respond: where else can we go to find life? We have tried everything else, and it has left us empty. We have heard all the words and noises of our culture, and they have proved false or only partially true. Where else would we go? We believe in you, Jesus, and we want to keep following you. Help us be loyal and faithful.

The Response of a Lead Follower

Sara Cobb is an active lay member of St. Luke's United Methodist Church in Indianapolis and is also the vice president for education with Lilly Endowment, Inc. She has chaired the Leadership Transition Team at St. Luke's in a time of transition from one senior pastor to the next. Here is her response:

> Over several months, six of us at St. Luke's worked closely with our bishop and district superintendent in discerning God's will during the transition to a new senior pastor. We spent considerable time in prayer, talked at length about Jesus and the guidance he offered in John 21:6, and reflected on a wonderful picture of Jesus in the room where we met. During that discernment process, we learned first-hand that change is hard. Just as the disciples experienced in John 6, a message that portends change is hard to hear. In this case, the message was a beloved senior pastor preparing for retirement and a committee working to seek a replacement. Some in the church chose to express discomfort with the process, focus, and potential outcome—perhaps even turning their backs, as some of the disciples did. We remained vigilant in our efforts and loyal to the abiding love, strength, and guidance provided by Jesus as we turned to him, our steadfast companion on our journey.
>
> Over the years, I have been challenged by professional, personal, spiritual, or physical decisions. Many of them have been hard; some outcomes have been disappointing; at times, I've felt alone in the effort to persevere; and occasionally, I have sought the advice of others. In the end, however, my loyalty always turns to Jesus. Prayer has

been my foundation, and Jesus has never once let me down. The transition at St. Luke's was no exception. Jesus was with us through the hard decisions, disappointments, and joys. In the end, we rest knowing we did not turn our backs on the One who led us through.

Reflect and Discuss

1. Are you loyal to Jesus?

2. Where else have you looked and tried to find answers in your life?

3. What is it about Jesus that keeps bringing you back to his words, his way, and his life?

4. Are you loyal to the Church that Jesus loves? And to other followers of Jesus?

5. Have you ever faced disloyalty or the diminishing of the crowds that Jesus faced? How did you maintain your own loyalty in the midst of the disloyalty of others?

Chapter Ten

Lead Followers Listen and Hear (John 14:8-9)

Good leaders share one common characteristic that is often overlooked in discussions about leadership: they know how to listen. They listen well, they use good listening skills, and they listen to the right people. They don't just listen to the "yes people" who surround some leaders; good leaders listen to their team, and they listen to their customers.

Such listening is not an easy task. We live in a noisy world, in which every moment and every space seems to be filled with noise, input, media, and opinions. In the midst of such a noisy environment, leaders have to work hard to listen.

I recently stayed in a hotel that had three flat-screen televisions in every elevator, each set to a different channel (sports, news, and some talk show), all blaring at the same time. What could possibly happen on any of those three channels that an elevator rider would not want to miss during the short ride up or down between floors? We are afraid of silence in our culture. We seemingly have to fill every space, every place, and every moment with sights and sounds. Consider how many teenagers fill their every waking moment with noise—some even sleep with their headphones blaring music in their ears. We adults do the same. Most households have televisions blaring all the time. Most of us drive our cars with the radio or other media blaring. Many people cannot jog or walk or mow the yard without listening to an iPod.

Leaders, especially good leaders, have to learn to listen in the midst of a noisy world.

Jesus Taught His Disciples to Listen and Hear

Lead Followers share the characteristic of listening, but they have an additional characteristic. They don't just listen; they also hear.

One theme of the Gospels is that Jesus used his teachings, especially his parables, to help his disciples learn to listen and to hear. He taught them to hear and discern hidden messages, deeper meanings, and more profound truths that the crowds missed. Here is a typical conclusion to a teaching passage from the Gospels: "With many such parables he continued to give them the word, as much as they were able to hear. He spoke to them only in parables, then explained everything to his disciples when he was alone with them" (Mark 4:33-34). Such moments are common in the Gospels, and it seems that Jesus taught his disciples to go beyond listening to hearing and understanding. He wanted his followers to perceive the truth of the kingdom of God, so he explained to them in private what was less obvious in public.

Even so, we have several examples of the disciples not listening well or understanding. One example is their inability to grasp some of the symbolism of Jesus' teachings. Matthew 16:5-7 tells a story in which the disciples misunderstood what Jesus meant by *bread*. Jesus' disciples had forgotten to bring any bread, so they had only one loaf with them in the boat. He gave them strict orders: "Watch out, be on guard for the yeast of the Pharisees as well as the yeast of Herod." The disciples discussed among themselves, "He said this because we have no bread" (paraphrased). Such moments are comical, as we see the inability of the disciples to listen and understand. Such moments must have been frustrating to Jesus, as they would be to any leader who is unable to get his followers to listen, hear, and understand.

Perhaps that is why many of the teachings of Jesus end with the admonition, "Whoever has ears to listen should pay attention!" (Mark 4:9). Jesus was calling for his followers to listen, hear, perceive, and understand. The Lead Followers of Jesus are persons who learn to listen at these deeper levels.

Listening to God

Jesus taught his Lead Followers to listen to God. He modeled a lifestyle of listening. It is interesting to read the Gospels and to notice the rhythm of the ministry of Jesus. He has times of intense activity, teaching, healing, challenging, sharing, laughing with friends, and engaging with those who were his enemies. Those intense times of engagement are often followed by times of disengagement, going off alone, praying, and listening to God.

A visit to the region of the Galilee makes it clear how Jesus used the beautiful geography of that region for this rhythmic pattern of listening and acting. Most of the small cities and villages of the Galilean region surround the beautiful lakeshore, so it is only a short walk up into the hillsides to get away from those gathering places. Often we read in the Gospels of Jesus going "up" to pray, which was the easiest way to withdraw from his active moments, to find silence and solace, and to listen to God.

We know that his disciples noticed how those times of listening to God empowered Jesus, for they asked him, "Lord, teach us to pray, just as John taught his disciples" (Luke 11:1). Note that this request came just after the disciples observed Jesus praying. There was something compelling about his example of praying and listening to God, which caused his disciples to ask him to teach them. Perhaps they wanted to have a rote prayer such as the one John the Baptist gave his disciples (and Jesus gave them and us such a prayer, the Lord's Prayer), but the context of their request makes it clear that they were asking for more than a set of words to memorize. The followers of Jesus saw the example of his listening to God, and they knew that they needed that pattern in order to be his followers, and especially to be his Lead Followers.

Lead Followers are persons who listen deeply to God to have a sense of direction, purpose, and mission. They continue the listening process with their team and to their "customers," or new people.

Listening to the Team

The best and most appreciated leaders have a knack for listening to their own team of leaders and followers. They know that they need input from those who are on the front line of their business or ministry, and they find ways to hear from their team.

During my years as district superintendent in Lafayette, Indiana, I heard an amazing story about Sam Walton, the founder of Walmart. It seems that Sam showed up at the Lafayette Walmart one day, unannounced, driving a modest pickup truck, and started working alongside the staff as they unpacked boxes and stocked shelves. He looked like he belonged; he knew what he was doing, so most of the workers simply accepted his participation. While they worked, he asked them a few open-ended questions, such as, "Do you enjoy working here?" and "How does the manager of the store treat you?" and even "Do you think these Walmart shoppers are getting a good deal?" He listened politely and carefully to the workers, and only later did he go to the front office to talk with the store managers. I heard this story from several persons who worked at Walmart, and they were amazed and pleased to learn that Sam himself had been with them, listening to them and their ideas. Apparently that was a pattern for most of Sam's life and work. What an example of a leader who listens!

Are you listening to your team? If you are a pastor, are you listening to your staff and your lay leadership? If you chair a committee or ministry team in your congregation, are you listening to those on your team? Is anyone listening to the custodian or the receptionist or the volunteers who quietly do their work? We in the church ought to be models of good listening, and those who want to be Lead Followers must learn to listen to their team.

As a pastor, I met regularly with each member of our church staff, one-on-one, usually in the staff member's office or place of ministry. Rather than having them come to my office, I found that meeting the staff on their "turf" set the right atmosphere for them to share and for me to listen. I also met at least yearly with the chair of every committee or team in the church, to listen to his or her concerns and ideas and to offer my help. During my years as district superintendent, I met with every pastor in my district in his or her church office, often concluding that meeting by praying with the pastor in his or her sanctuary. Now as a bishop, I meet regularly with every district superintendent, with every director on our conference staff, and with key lay leaders in the conference.

The context of all of those meetings is the same: it is about listening to the team members. My usual agenda (which they receive in advance) includes these simple questions:

- How is it with your soul? How is your own life with God?
- How is your family? Any special concerns or needs of your family that I can pray for?
- How is your ministry going? Share with me whatever you want to share.
- How can I help you to do a better job with your ministry?
- What do I need to know that I am not hearing?

Those simple questions have been my way of opening up a time for listening and also hearing from my team members. Listening is one of the ways that a leader is empowered by the followers or team members. If leadership is indeed a product of the group or congregation or team, then one of the ways the members of the team empower their leader is when they know they can share openly and honestly with that leader and be heard. A leader who listens to the followers is given great authority by those followers to lead. That is why Lead Followers must listen and hear.

Listening to New People

In addition to listening to God and listening to one's team members, excellent leaders also listen to their "customers," or to the new people being reached by their ministry. One can learn a great deal from listening to those who are the newest to a congregation, group, or business. What brought them here? Were we hospitable to them? How did we almost miss them? What new ideas or dreams can they offer to us?

While working on my Doctor of Ministry project through Drew Theological Seminary, I did a research project to study new members of congregations and to learn why they joined (this unpublished study is titled *Why People Join* and is available from Drew Theological Seminary. Some of the results of that study are also included in the book that I coauthored with Douglas Anderson, *The Race to Reach Out* (Nashville: Abingdon Press, 2004). I learned many fascinating facts about new members, and especially I learned that our response to new persons must be based upon two qualities: timing and listening.

Most of the new members told stories about visiting other churches and having no response or a very slow response. After those new persons had made the effort to overcome their fears about church people and to visit a church, receiving no response or a slow response came across as rude and uncaring. Typically we found that a response within the first seventy-two hours was most effective. Waiting several days or even a week meant that the visitor was unlikely ever to return. The irony here, of course, is that many mainline or "oldline" Protestant congregations and ministers don't want to be "pushy," and therefore they don't respond until visitors have come two or three Sundays. My research found that taking that approach is ineffective with most new people.

The other quality that new members reported they needed was listening. They were not impressed with churches or ministers who tried to "sell them" on their church. Rather, these new persons wanted a prompt response that was caring and friendly, and they wanted to be contacted by people who were willing to listen to them. Typically this meant a friendly phone call or later an actual visit in person by trained visitors who know how to listen to the needs, hopes, hurts, and dreams of new people.

What's more, once a new person becomes an actual participant or member of a congregation, my research showed that they wanted to be included, involved, and asked for their input. Many of these new persons have amazing stories to tell and wonderful contributions to make, if only we will ask, listen, and include them.

It's a Matter of Integrity

In spite of the inability of many of Jesus' followers to hear and understand all of the implications of his teachings, they found his teaching to have authority—the authority of integrity. Note this passage from the Gospel of Matthew: "When Jesus finished these words, the crowds were amazed at his teaching because he was teaching them like someone with authority and not like their legal experts" (Matt. 7:28-29). What was the nature of this "authority" of Jesus? I believe it was his integrity.

Integrity means "oneness" or "wholeness" of person, message, action, and life. Jesus taught with the authority of a person who was consistent, honest, whole, and complete. Such integrity is another characteristic of a Lead Follower who listens and hears.

How does a Lead Follower show integrity? By listening well, by being authentic in words and actions, and by being consistent. A good leader, and especially a Lead Follower, never says one thing in a meeting and another thing in the "meeting after the meeting" in the parking lot or the next day at the coffee shop. A Lead Follower of Jesus models his or her life after the kind of wholeness that Jesus lived. A Lead Follower of Jesus is known by his or her "word" being good.

An example of integrity in my upbringing was my grandfather. He was always kind, generous, loving, and caring. He always followed through on what he said he would do. As a young kid, I could see the difference between my grandfather's integrity and some of the examples of other adults who would tell us kids one thing and then do another. Or worse, I would see some adults who would act one way around us kids but then be an entirely different person around other adults.

My grandfather lived with an integrity that gained notice. He grew up on a farm but decided to move to town (a small town of 600 people) and open his own service station, then later a meat locker, and various other businesses. He gained such respect for his honesty and integrity that when the bank from the county seat wanted to open a branch in this town, my grandfather was hired as the bank manager. At first he protested that he did not know anything about banking, but the bankers from the county seat said, "That's all right. We can teach you the banking business. We need a local leader who has the trust of the people." My grandfather thus shifted careers and was a bank manager the last twenty-five years of his working life.

At his funeral, which occurred when I was a young pastor, I heard story after story from local townsfolk who praised the integrity of my grandfather. Many shared that he had made them loans when no one else would, seldom requiring much paperwork, but developing a basic trust that caused them never to default on their loans. They praised his sensitivity, his willingness to listen, and his desire to help them succeed. In a word: integrity.

Lead Followers of Jesus live their lives with the same integrity that Jesus modeled. Henri Nouwen helps us understand what that means. He says that to be Christlike is not to be a photocopy of Jesus, not to mimic Jesus, and not to try to be Jesus. Rather, he says, "to be Christ-like is to live my life as authentically as Jesus lived his life" (*The Living Reminder* [New York: Harper-Collins, 1977]). It means to live my life with integrity, just as Jesus modeled that integrity for his followers. Doing so will help me be a Lead Follower of Jesus.

An Inquiry from Jesus

"Don't you know me, Philip, even after I have been with you all this time?" (John 14:9).

Jesus asked this question in response to Philip's request to see the Father. Philip's request seems more than just a curiosity; it seems like a demand, something like, "Prove yourself, Jesus. Show us the Father, and then we will believe you are sent from him."

With sadness or exasperation, Jesus says, "Whoever has seen me has seen the Father" (John 14:9). Jesus indicates that there is integrity and oneness with God that permeate his own life. And then Jesus goes on to tell his followers that they will become Lead Followers: "I assure you that whoever believes in me will do the works that I do. They will do even greater works than these because I am going to the Father. I will do whatever you ask for in my name, so that the Father can be glorified in the Son. When you ask me for anything in my name, I will do it" (John 14:12-14). With those words and his subsequent action in sending the Spirit to empower his disciples, Jesus transformed his disciples into Lead Followers.

The Response of a Lead Follower

Douglas Anderson is the executive director of the Bishop Rueben Job Center for Leadership Development. In that role and in other experiences he is an expert church consultant who listens to congregations and helps diagnose their issues. Here is his response:

Bishop Coyner has identified the three critical foci of listening for effective leaders in the church, including pastors. The central focus of listening as a leader is to God. Spending time listening to what God is saying to us through Scripture and in prayer helps clarify God's direction for us, as well as deepens our humility to set aside our own agenda for God's leading. Listening deeply to God also gives us the courage to act when it is difficult or uncomfortable. Jesus consistently models this deep listening to God.

Another focus of listening as a leader is to others in the church. I have discovered this is best accomplished by asking good, open-ended questions to learn from the other persons. Asking questions further demonstrates our respect for them and their opinion, as well as builds mutual trust—key factors for leading. Good leaders seek to listen more than tell.

The third focus of leader listening is newcomers. There is no better way of demonstrating the gospel than through caring enough truly to listen to newcomers. From intentional listening, we can discern how to connect them through participation in ministries and small groups that fit their gifts and spiritual path. We can assist where God is leading them rather than simply push where we need them to go.

Listening is the most critical process for effective leadership. The better we listen to God, to others in the church, and to newcomers, the better leaders we will become.

Reflect and Discuss

1. Does your leadership style include listening to God, listening to your team, and listening to new people?

2. Are you comfortable with the notion that being "Christlike" is not about mimicking Christ but about living your life as authentically as he lived his? Why or why not?

3. Does being a Lead Follower place more demands upon you, or does it give you a greater sense of freedom?

4. Do you feel "assured" by Jesus that you will do even greater works than he has done?

5. What else do you need from Jesus to be one of his Lead Followers? Can you follow his instruction and "ask in his name" for whatever you need?

Chapter Eleven

Lead Followers Lead the Leader (John 21:15-17)

Being a Lead Follower is about following the Lordship of Jesus and the leadership of other Christians, but sometimes it is also about leading the leader. "Leading the leader" is a recognized, accepted, and valued concept from the business and sports world. It is common in basketball, for example, to see the head coach listening to assistant coaches share what they are seeing, hearing, and thinking during the first part of a timeout. Only after listening to the assistant coaches will these effective head coaches turn to their team and give instructions. What is the role of those assistant coaches? It is leading the leader. Likewise, many business experts today advocate "leading from the second chair" or "leading from behind" or "managing your boss." Some of those concepts relate to the idea of being a Lead Follower—one who can lead the leader and help the leader fulfill the mission of the organization. At its best, "leading the leader" does not mean manipulating the leader; rather, it means offering new options for the leader to choose or not choose, and it is the very wise leader who listens to those followers who are helping the leader lead.

Leading the Leader in Church

Why is it that we so seldom value that concept in the Christian community? Why do we not see that an excellent Lead Follower can also help lead the leader? Perhaps we in the church are still functioning on outdated business leadership models, whereas most excellent businesses have moved forward and developed concepts of team leadership. The church, of all places, should be a place where the role of Lead Follower can mean helping lead the leader.

I remember well a lay leader in one of my churches—a man named Kent—who understood the role of leading the leader. One day Kent called and offered to take me to lunch. Over lunch he said, "Pastor Mike, everyone in the church loves you and respects your leadership, but that makes it hard for us to tell you when you are wrong. I asked you to lunch today to tell you that you are wrong on this issue and that you need to rethink it." I have long forgotten what the particular issue was, but I have never forgotten the friendship, love, support, and honesty of Kent, who cared enough about my leadership and me to tell me the truth. I am sure that the issue was some unrealistic or ill-planned idea of mine, and Kent saved me from the frustration of trying to lead my congregation in a direction that they were unwilling to go. Although some laity might challenge their pastoral leaders in an unhealthy power struggle, Kent's approach was caring, supportive, and encouraging. Sometimes "leading the leader" means being the Lead Follower who will speak the truth in love.

Likewise, I can remember a staff member in another church who came to me and said, "The whole church is waiting for you to tackle this issue. You can do it in two or three different ways, but we are all stuck until you lead us." Again, I don't remember what the issue was, but I do remember that staff person making me aware that the body needed my leadership. Sometimes "leading the leader" means pushing a leader off dead center to make a decision.

Still today I value close friends and colleagues who tell me the truth, invite me to lead, and help me consider options. Not everyone will do that for a bishop in our United Methodist Church, but it sure helps me. One friend comes around every few months and asks me some open-ended questions that help me lead. He never has an agenda, other than helping me think through my options. He may ask, for example, "I know you really care about helping our congregations reach outside their walls in ministry, so what new ways are you planning to communicate that to our congregations?" His questions get me thinking, and we often talk about some possibilities, and then he leaves me with the choices to make because he is clear that he is not the bishop. However, he is excellent at "leading the leader."

Leaders Welcome Reminders about Their Mission

One of the characteristics of Lead Followers is that they welcome help in leading.

Even Jesus himself received and welcomed that help. This book considers inquiries from Jesus, but one of the inquiries made to Jesus came from John the Baptist. In Luke 7:18-20 we read that John sent his messengers to Jesus to ask him, "Are you the one who is coming, or should we look for someone else?" Some scholars and interpreters have seen this question from John the Baptist as an indication that he was getting discouraged (he was in prison after all, and he was near to being executed by Herod) or that John had begun to have doubts about Jesus.

What if the point of John's question was to "lead the leader" and to help his cousin Jesus clarify and articulate his mission? It is noteworthy that the response of Jesus is in fact the "mission statement" that he uses throughout his ministry. Jesus tells those messengers to go back to John and report: "Those who were blind are able to see. Those who were crippled now walk. People with skin diseases are cleansed. Those who were deaf now hear. Those who were dead are raised up. And good news is preached to the poor. Happy is anyone who doesn't stumble along the way because of me" (Luke 7:22-23). This answer of Jesus is the same message or mission statement that he announced in his hometown of Nazareth, when he quoted Isaiah's promise, "The Spirit of the Lord is upon me, / because the Lord has anointed me. / He has sent me to preach good news to the poor, / to proclaim release to the prisoners / and recovery of sight to the blind, / to liberate the oppressed, / and to proclaim the year of the Lord's favor" (Luke 4:18-19). Jesus followed the prophet Isaiah by claiming that he was himself the fulfillment of Isaiah's prophecy.

John's question to Jesus was that of a good follower who had also been the predecessor of Jesus to prepare the way for him. He is asking a question to lead the leader. He asks his question perhaps already knowing what the answer will be. He is reminding Jesus to claim his mission and to fulfill his calling because people are looking for "the One." Jesus apparently not only welcomed that question but also used that occasion to tell his own disciples about the important role that John the Baptist had played in his own calling. Jesus dares to compare John to Elijah, or at least he says that John has played the Elijah role. There is not much higher praise one could give to John the Baptist, who was both Jesus' predecessor and his Lead Follower.

John the Baptist is quite clear about his own role as a Lead Follower of Jesus, as one who prepares the way, but who knows that another is coming "who is more powerful than me...I'm not worthy to loosen the strap of his sandals" (Luke 3:16). John sees himself as the one who prepares the way for the One who is coming, and in that role he demonstrates the best characteristics of a Lead Follower.

Jesus not only accepts John's role (after all, he had allowed John to baptize him) but also receives John's question, "Are you the one?" without any sense of insult or outrage. Instead, prompted by that question, Jesus quietly repeats his mission statement and tells those messengers to go back to John and tell him, in essence, "Yes, I remember my mission. Thanks for the chance to articulate it again." I can even imagine Jesus smiling with appreciation that John had once again played his role of "leading the leader."

I Have Been Reminded of My Mission As a Leader

I can relate to that situation in a small and humble way, having been blessed by people who have played this "leading the leader" role with me by reminding me of my own mission. I remember a church secretary named Bill who led me often. Bill was a retired businessman who was hired by the congregation to serve as church secretary, not because he was a great typist, but because he was a great organizer of details. When I arrived as pastor, at age twenty-nine, Bill became a person who often was able to "lead the leader." He would say to me many times a week, "I am here to help you with the details so that you are free to establish your ministry. You are the pastor, so just tell me what things you need organized, and I will take care of the details." What a wonderful gift he was, and how beautifully he was able to "lead the leader."

Today as a bishop, I am blessed with several persons on my staff and in my life who are great at "leading the leader," and they often do so by asking me the kind of question that John the Baptist asked Jesus. One in particular will ask me, "Well, you are the bishop, aren't you?" It is a way of nudging me to claim my authority and leadership because he understands that if I will not lead, then no one else can do my job for me.

My examples are humble and trite by comparison, but they perhaps illustrate the message of John to Jesus: "Be the One you are called be. Don't worry about me in prison; I am okay, just keep doing what God has called you to do." John the Baptist was leading the leader, and Jesus was able to accept his support. Every good leader should follow his example.

Can We Remind One Another of Our Mission?

In the life of the church, can we create a sense of team leadership in which we "dance" between being a leader and a follower, and in which we remind one another to follow our mission of being followers of Jesus? Can we find ways to ask one another the kinds of inquiries that Jesus used to guide and teach his disciples? Can we use the practice of "leading the leader" to help one another lead?

Here is what it might look like if our ministry team and committee meetings happened within an environment of leading and following: perhaps the elected or chosen leader of the group would start each session by reminding the group of its mission, and then one of the other members would offer devotions and prayer to continue to focus upon the mission. The session could continue with each member "leading" the part of the agenda for which each is responsible, while the elected leader would take a step back into a "leading the leader" role as a follower. But the whole group would also take part in asking the kinds of inquiries that Jesus made, in order to help keep the group moving forward in its mission. One member might ask, for example, "That sounds like a great project, but how will it help us accomplish our purpose?" By working in an environment of team leadership, the dance between leading and following could be quite smooth and flowing. Trying to describe it is artificial and stilted, and it may take practice for a group or team to develop a smooth flow, but such a "dance" can be a beautiful thing to see.

"Leading the leader" is an important skill for the Lead Follower, but it is worth the practice and the effort if it helps the entire group, team, committee, or congregation move effectively and efficiently toward its mission.

An Inquiry from Jesus

"Do you love me?" (John 21:15-17).

Jesus asked this question three times of Simon Peter in one of the most interesting post-Easter stories, recorded in John 21:15-17. Just as Peter had three times denied Jesus, Jesus asks Peter the question three times. In each case after Peter claims to love Jesus, Jesus tells him, "Feed my lambs...take care of my sheep...feed my sheep." At that moment, Jesus actually became the one who was leading the leader by commissioning Peter to be a leader. Oftentimes, true leadership is observed in such times of "passing the mantle" to one's successor and leading that leader.

The Response of a Lead Follower

Brian Durand is Associate Director for Leadership Development of the Indiana Conference. In that role he leads, nurtures, and supports leaders. Here is his response:

> As I reflect on the concept of "leading the leader," I'm struck by what this perspective offers to the leadership conversation in churches. Often as I hear leadership discussed, the concept is that one leader has to get out of the way for a new one to assume the leadership role.

This understanding is threatening to current leaders and daunting to new leaders. Leading the leader invites us to consider a model of shared leadership, one reflective of our understanding of the body of Christ. A current leader can empower a new leader to take the lead where gifts and passions connect, while a new leader through questions and input can contribute to the decisions and missional focus of the current team leader.

It strikes me that this "dance" of leadership sharing is not an easy task, however. For Peter, having his future mission clarified through a reference to his past could not have been easy. For us as leaders, accepting challenges to our intended decisions and direction while allowing followers to lead us can be tough. For us as followers, challenging a pending decision or saying what we believe can be daunting on a team. Diligently developing a sense of shared mission and deep trust is a challenge for many teams. And yet, when I encounter church teams in my ministry that have a true sense of shared leadership as followers of Christ, the fruit of their ministry is amazing. The effort to perfect the "dance" of leading the leader is worth it, as leading and loving together in leadership feeds our community and world.

Reflect and Discuss

1. Evidently Jesus sees a strong connection among loving and leading and feeding. People who are fed, loved, cared for, valued, and protected are people who are willing to be led. Many so-called leaders are not able to feel or express to their people a deep love for them by feeding them. Do you love and feed the people you try to lead?

2. How do you think Peter felt when Jesus asked him three times, "Do you love me?"

3. Was Jesus "leading the leader" for Peter when he asked those questions about feeding his sheep? If so, how?

4. As a leader, do you listen to the leading of your followers who may be trying to lead the leader? Who are the persons who are trying to lead you to be a better leader? Who are the leaders who need your help in leading them to lead?

5. Do you love Jesus?

Chapter Twelve

Lead Followers Pay the Price
(Mark 10:38-40)

Being a Lead Follower can be costly, and those of us who follow Jesus and who follow other Christian leaders must be prepared to pay that price by yielding our egos, by being willing to be incorrect, and by accepting our share of responsibility even when we do not receive our share of the credit.

Paying the Price of Ego

One of my pastor friends says that *ego* means "edging God out" of our lives. He can't remember the source of that quote, and I suspect it is not original with him, but it is a truth nonetheless. When our own ego gets in the way, it is easy for us to edge God out of our lives, our decision-making, and our leadership. Excellent leaders learn to put their own ego aside for the sake of the mission of their group, congregation, or business. Ineffective leaders try to lead from their own ego, their own gifts, and their own desire to be in charge.

The term *Lead Follower* used in this book is a way of reminding all leaders that our first task is to put our ego aside and to follow Jesus and other Christian leaders. True leadership is not about us as individuals; it is about the mission. True leadership is a willingness to take a backseat at times and to allow others to lead. True leadership is not concerned with who gets credit. True leadership is about paying the price of our own ego for the higher purpose of the group, congregation, business, or movement. That is what is meant by the term *Lead Follower*.

Many would-be leaders are unsuccessful because their ego gets in the way. I watched a new senior pastor come into a large, well-run church with an excellent staff and nearly dismantle the staff and ministry within two years. What was his problem? He could not allow others to receive credit, even when it was obvious to the congregation that another staff person had birthed the idea, done the work, and deserved the credit.

By contrast I have watched excellent CEOs and excellent senior pastors who lead and gain trust from their staffs by yielding their own egos. One CEO in particular, whose work I observe as a board member, is always quick to invite staff into our meetings to share their success stories, following which he gives them their due praise in front of the board. It is no surprise to hear these staff persons offer a strong sense of loyalty, not just to the CEO, but to the mission of the organization.

Being an effective leader often means paying the price of releasing one's own ego. In the same way, being a Lead Follower and serving on a staff or on a team also means paying the price of releasing one's own ego. I spoke recently with an effective associate pastor and asked him the secret to his effective ministry. His answer is worth repeating: "I believe my job is to make my senior pastor look good. Not everyone has a strong enough ego to do that, but I find it is a very meaningful ministry."

Meekness Is Not Weakness

The words of that associate pastor remind us that in the Bible *meekness* is not another word for *weakness*. Rather, *meekness* is about strength harnessed and directed to a higher cause. The Greek word for *meekness,* which is used to translate the teachings of Jesus on this subject, is the same Greek word used to describe a powerful stallion that is well trained to serve his master. Meekness in any biblical sense is not about weakness but about strength, power, ego, and skill that are directed in service.

A Lead Follower who pays the price of setting aside his or her own ego is not a doormat to be tromped upon by others. Simply allowing others to push us around, to demean our work, to criticize us unfairly, or to steal credit for our ministry is not what meekness is about.

In many ways it requires more strength, more ego strength, more skill, and a stronger sense of personhood for us to take the role of Lead Follower and to allow others to lead. Serving on a team—whether it be a ministry team or a business team—requires greater strength, not weakness; but it requires paying the price of setting aside individual egotistical needs for the mission of the group.

Paying the Price of Being Correct

Many leaders in the church today preach about God's grace and forgiveness and second chances but then operate their ministry as if we dare not be incorrect. Some would-be leaders cannot lead because they worry too much about always being (or appearing to be) correct. Where is the "grace" that we preach?

Ronald Heifetz makes this point so well in his book *Leadership Without Easy Answers*. He points to our desire to be correct, to have the proper answers, and to be in charge as indications of poor leadership. Leadership today, he argues, must be a leadership that is willing to raise the crucial questions without always having the correct answers.

Perhaps it would be helpful to look at this issue from the other side. What if being a leader means always being correct? Who is eligible for that job description? Even if a leader is correct most of the time, what followers would find it fulfilling to follow such a leader? Isn't part of the joy of leading and following the very fact that we need one another? Is there not some genuine value in allowing the whole group to fly higher, faster, and further than any individual can do?

The story called "A Lesson from Geese" has made its way around the Internet, sometimes with beautiful photography of geese flying in typical V formation. The story points to the scientific fact that a flock of geese can fly further than any goose flying alone. The story also points to the special role of honking to encourage the lead goose, how the leader of the flying formation changes periodically, and how the flock assigns two geese to help out any goose that becomes sick and needs to drop out. We can learn a lot about shared leadership from geese.

We can also learn a lot about the false bravado of our need to be "correct" from a simple exercise that I have seen conducted with groups. Take a common object, such as a paper cup, and give everyone in the group ninety seconds to write down all of the ways a paper cup can be used. Then have someone share his or her answers, and allow others to keep adding any new answers. The total group will come up with two to three times the number of total answers of any one person. Why? Because none of us is truly "correct" on our own. We need one another.

Leaders, especially Lead Followers, are willing to pay the price of yielding their notion of being correct. That willingness allows the total group to move ahead faster and farther.

I watched one effective senior pastor of a large congregation exemplify this truth during his ministry. He often had trouble even telling visitors the titles of his staff, which would prompt him to say, "I am not really sure what [name] is doing. I just know a good leader when I see one, and I try to stay out of their way." He also fumbled some when he tried to quote statistics or to share about new programs or ministries, with his own staff having to correct him. I think in some ways he was a Columbo-type of leader—that TV detective who feigned lack of knowledge to keep asking good questions of suspects—but the pastor certainly was able to yield any sense of being correct in order to further the mission of his team. And he was a beloved leader.

It's okay to be wrong. It is okay to be uniformed. It is okay to allow others to correct us. It is okay to be willing to share the credit. And it is okay to be human. Most good leaders have those faults, and they use them to allow the whole team to exert stronger leadership.

Being a Lead Follower means we are not always correct.

Paying the Price of Success

Lead Followers are willing to risk and fail, if it can lead to future victories for the team's mission.

One of my district superintendents reported to our cabinet meeting a few years ago, "I have had several important failures recently." His report surprised our team, but he went on to explain that he had tried some new ministries and projects that had failed but that he had learned from those failures and was now ready to try new efforts. He called those "important failures" as a way of reminding us that we must fail once in a while if we are going to learn how to succeed.

This is another price that many leaders are not willing to pay. They will study, hesitate, study some more, delay, avoid, and refine a planned effort until they are certain it cannot possibly fail. Often those very delays and refinements mean the opportunity has been missed. Often they have created such fear that the group is unwilling to take a risk. And often they have set the bar for "success" so low that even when an effort succeeds it is virtually meaningless.

Why are we so afraid to risk, to try, to fail sometimes, but to learn? Are we once again preaching grace but practicing a kind of "works righteousness" with our leadership? Compare these two congregations: Grace Church decided to improve their congregation's participation in Bible study, so they launched three new Bible study classes. After about three months, they concluded that one class was doing better than expected, one was struggling and needed some help, and the third had already quit meeting because of low attendance. Meanwhile, Faith Church wanted to avoid those kinds of problems, so they have been studying all of the best ways to launch a new Bible study class, they have sent potential leaders to various workshops and training events, and they are developing a plan to launch a new class once they have all of those potential problems resolved ahead of time. Which congregation is doing a better job of improving their participation in Bible study? Obviously is it Grace Church, and obviously this example is overstated, but not by much. Too many leaders and too many congregations are afraid to fail, so they never succeed. Lead Followers are willing to risk, to try, to fail, to learn, and to try again.

A willingness to risk failure is especially true for Lead Followers who already are leading a good team. Jim Collins, in *From Good to Great* (New York: Harper Collins, 2001), says that "good is the enemy of great." We get so comfortable with being a "good" team, business, congregation, or group that we become unwilling to risk the new efforts that can help us become "great." He further says that excellent leaders work on their "stop doing" lists rather than just keep a busy schedule with lots of "to do" lists. Excellent leaders are always asking themselves, "What do I need to stop doing and let go, in order to put my energy and focus on some new endeavor that may help us improve and succeed?"

What Does Success Look Like?

Perhaps it would help us pay the price of "success" and risk failure if we had a better perspective on the true meaning of success. To put it bluntly: we follow a Jesus who did not "succeed" by many of the typical measures of success. He risked failure by the typical measures in favor of a higher purpose. Jesus probably never traveled more than about one hundred miles from his place of birth and his upbringing. He had virtually no possessions, other than a robe that his executioners gambled to claim. He had friends and followers, but most of them deserted him when he was arrested, convicted, and executed. Certainly the power groups and authorities of his day saw him as a failure. His only "title" mocked him from above the cross where he died. He was buried in a borrowed tomb. Was Jesus a failure? How do we define *success* in the face of the Gospel story of Jesus?

When I hear potential leaders—laity and clergy—worry about their own success and the success of their congregations and groups, I seldom hear them worrying about the same issues that seemed to dominate the life and witness of Jesus. Membership statistics, budgets, salary packages, recognition in the community, awards from civic groups, approval from their colleagues, personal pension accounts, and even their health and safety—those points of worry for most leaders seem not to have been on the mind or the priority list of Jesus. By those standards, Jesus' life and ministry did not succeed.

Perhaps we who follow Jesus would be less fearful of failure and more willing to learn from our "important failures" if we focused upon a different meaning of *success.*

A Successful Lead Follower

A successful Lead Follower listens to God, listens to his or her team, listens to new people, and then makes decisions based upon his or her best hunch about how to achieve the mission of the group. A successful Lead Follower is willing to play second fiddle, to give credit to those other persons who deserve credit, and then to meekly offer his or her own best strengths for the team and its mission. A successful Lead Follower invites potential new followers to become leaders, too, and offers them support, encouragement, freedom, and resources to lead in their own way. Successful Lead Followers measure their own life and witness after the example of Jesus, and not after the measurements of the world. Successful Lead Followers gladly pay whatever price is required to follow Jesus, to follow other Christian leaders, and to lead their team to be faithful to Jesus.

An Inquiry from Jesus

"Can you drink the cup I drink or receive the baptism I receive?" (Mark 10:38).

Jesus answered James and John when they wanted a special place in the kingdom. Jesus was amazingly patient with them when they misunderstood discipleship and wanted it to include privileges. Jesus was amazingly patient with all of the disciples when they argued about who was the greatest. And Jesus was amazingly honest when he offered his potential followers a tough life, filled with suffering, sacrifice, and even death.

Jesus did ask those followers, and he asks us, "Are you able to pay the price?"

The Response of a Lead Follower

Adolf Hansen is a retired professor of theology and a regular consultant with a variety of seminaries, congregations, and other leadership groups. He also cochaired the Imagine Indiana Team that helped form the new Indiana Conference from the former North and South Conferences. Here is his response:

> Yes, it's costly to be a Lead Follower, especially a Lead Follower of Jesus. Yet it's worth it! For it satisfies Lead Followers at the depth of their being. This doesn't mean it's easy, but it does mean it fulfills what God intended. My experience confirms this—unequivocally!
>
> I have learned if I continually seek to bring honor to God, my ego is not as prominent in my life. However, knowing that is easier than actualizing it. I have also learned if I pose or invite inquiring questions, and then share my best thinking at a given point in time—though not necessarily my final conclusions—I am more open, more inclusive of other persons' contributions, and more creative. Doing this by sending up trial balloons, by sharing what seems to be, and by expressing my thoughts as honestly as I can helps me lessen the need always to be correct. In addition, I have learned that success is not fully perceived ahead of time but is a developmental realization of a worthy goal, something that emerges through reflection, sharing, and being unafraid to take risks—even to fail. And it takes place most meaningfully when a group takes ownership, acts on it, and receives recognition as a team.
>
> Yet there is a more profound price to pay. For, when Jesus asks his question, "Can *you* drink the cup...," he is clearly referring to his anticipated suffering—identified and explained three times in Mark (8:27–9:1; 9:30-37; 10:32-45). Jesus is asking his followers, especially his Lead Followers, if they are willing to pay the price—willing to suffer, even to the point of death.
>
> Dietrich Bonhoeffer captures this understanding in his penetrating words: "When Christ calls a man, he bids him come and die."

Reflect and Discuss

1. What price have you paid in order to follow Jesus?

2. Do you agree that *meekness* has often been misunderstood as *weakness* in the Christian tradition? If so, why do you think that is true?

3. What kind of ego strength does it require to be a follower of Jesus or to allow other Christians to lead us?

4. Where have you risked being incorrect or pursuing what might end up as a failure in your ministry? What did you learn from those experiences?

5. Are you able and willing to pay the price to be a Lead Follower?

conclusion

You Can Be a Lead Follower
(Matthew 14:29-31)

You can be a Lead Follower. Jesus calls us to be his disciples or followers, but he also helps us become leaders. Jesus and his disciples provide the model for a leader who leads but who also invites others to lead and who allows them to be Lead Followers.

Following Jesus is about becoming a Lead Follower, one who both follows and leads. Being a Lead Follower takes practice, skill development, and a new way of living and leading. You can do that. You can be a Lead Follower. It starts with following Jesus, but then it moves into areas of learned behaviors and attitudes. Here are ten simple ways to become a Lead Follower.

Listen Well

One of the characteristics of a Lead Follower listed in chapter 10 is "listening and hearing." It was further indicated that a Lead Follower must listen to God, listen to the team, and listen to new people. Those listening skills and practices are essential for any good leader or follower, and they are first on this list of the ways to become a Lead Follower.

Too many people and too many books about leadership focus upon what the leader should say: how to share one's vision, how to communicate, how to use the media, and how to speak. All of that is secondary to the first step of listening. Part of the reason for listening is very practical: it earns one the right to speak. Being a good listener is such an unusual characteristic in today's world that the would-be leader who actually listens will garner enormous support and opportunity to lead. Another part of the reason for listening, of course, is that others have much to say from which we can learn. Listening also demonstrates love in a tangible and powerful way. Consider the famous "love chapter" of 1 Corinthians 13, which many see as the height of poetic expression about the power of love. Try reading that same chapter and exchanging the word *listening* for the word *love*. It fits! Love is perhaps best demonstrated through listening.

91

To become a Lead Follower, you must listen. Listen to God, listen to others, and also listen to your own heart.

Pray Constantly

The second way to become a Lead Follower is to pray constantly. Part of praying is listening to God, but part of praying is also talking to God. A Lead Follower is one who is in constant dialogue with God.

One of the most effective senior pastors I have known is a person who commits one hour a day to prayer. Some people talk about the importance of prayer, but he really does it! If you call his office in the morning during his prayer time, you will be told by his secretary, "I am sorry but the pastor is in prayer and cannot be disturbed." Somehow that message is reassuring to the caller. Rather than feeling put off or ignored by such a message, a caller feels encouraged to know that the pastor is in a prayerful relationship with God.

By contrast, what message is sent by the would-be leader who is constantly busy with meetings, details, and office work? Even though that person might be available to take a phone call, the caller might get the feeling this would-be leader is unable to offer any perspective or reply based upon a thorough and complete relationship with God.

If you want to be a Lead Follower, then pray constantly, and your leadership will be founded on prayerful practice.

Laugh Often

Lead Followers laugh often, mostly at themselves. Our model is Jesus, who told stories, enjoyed meals with his disciples and all kinds of folk, and apparently laughed often.

One of my favorite drawings of Jesus is called "Jesus Laughing." It was available in a children's Sunday school curriculum many years ago, and I have seen it in many church buildings. I think people are attracted to it because we need to know that Jesus was not always stern or "religious." Jesus enjoyed life, and that probably means he enjoyed a good laugh.

I know of a church council that met in a children's Sunday school room because of remodeling going on throughout their building. On the agenda that evening was the choice of new carpet for their remodeling, and evidently the discussion became quite heated between those who wanted green carpeting versus those who wanted blue. Suddenly one woman looked on the bulletin board in that classroom and saw the picture of Jesus laughing, and she began laughing hysterically at the thought of her church arguing about carpet choices. People demanded an explanation for her laughter, and it was all she could do to catch her breath and point to the picture. Everyone else began laughing, too, and after a good laugh they easily resolved their carpet-color choice.

Lead Followers laugh a lot, including seeing the humor in our human frailties and allowing good humor to move a group forward. One of the most helpful things leaders can do is to be human, to laugh at themselves, and to allow the group to have a little fun while doing the serious work of ministry.

Ask the Right Questions

This book has used a variety of "Inquiries from Jesus" but has only scratched the surface of his list of questions. Jesus constantly asks questions in the Gospels, and he uses his inquiries to make the points that are not always so obvious by declarative sentences. A Lead Follower knows that asking questions in a nonjudging way can open people's minds and hearts in ways that overcome their defensiveness.

What are the "right" questions? They are questions about the mission and purpose of the congregation, group, or organization. An excellent leader may ask, for example, "I have noticed that we always do this [naming a practice], and I am curious to know how that practice helps us accomplish our mission?" Or a leader may say, "Help me understand. Our purpose statement is very clear about this [naming a value]. How does that statement guide us on this project?" Such "right questions" are never asked to embarrass or to condemn, but rather they are open-ended and lead to further reflection.

I recall a lay leader in one of the churches I served who was excellent at asking questions. At one church council meeting, the missions team reported that their plans were set for the annual ice cream social for missions. He simply asked, "How much money do we typically raise for missions?" When the answer came back, "Not much, but we always have a lot of fun at that event," he replied, "Then should we call it a fellowship event rather than a missions event?" His questions led to a long discussion about the difference between events for us in the church, events for the community, and fund-raising events. We decided to go ahead with the ice cream social, invite the community to join us, and to include a kind of "missions fair," in which everyone could sign up to participate in various mission outreach opportunities—some sponsored by our church, and some sponsored by other community groups. That event was transformed into a new model for involving people in ministry, all because a lay leader asked some good questions.

A Lead Follower is one who asks the right questions.

Recruit Carefully

Jesus recruited and called his disciples carefully, and even then he ended up with a Judas. Lead Followers carefully recruit those who will serve on their team. An excellent team is not filled with a bunch of clones of the leader; rather, it is a balanced group, with a variety of gifts and skills.

Good recruiting takes time and discernment. My business-consultant brother-in-law says, "No amount of training can fix a bad hire." What should a Lead Follower seek in recruiting team members? First, a commitment to the mission is essential. Second, look for a person who can be both a leader and a follower. Third, choose only persons who are team players. Finally, recruit persons who complement the leader's gifts.

Delegate, Don't Dump or Dictate

Having recruited a team, too many would-be leaders decide that they should "delegate" the work to the various team members. However, their use of the word *delegate* often means everything from dictating the details of the work to simply dumping the work on a team member. Delegation is a continuum from "dictating," or clearly defining each step of the task, to "dumping," or simply giving an assignment to a trusted team member who needs little or no guidance. Delegation is the fine art of knowing what each team member needs from you as the leader. Typically a new team member doing a task for the first time will need lots of guidance and supervision, with perhaps with some practice role-playing before he or she can handle the task. An experienced team member may not want or need much supervision, and to offer too much supervision feels like an indication of the leader's lack of trust. Delegate carefully.

Here is a simple model for healthy delegation: "I do it, I do it with your help, you do it with my help, and then you do it."

A Lead Follower is one who knows how and when to delegate to the team members in order to allow them to become Lead Followers too.

Be Lavish in Giving Credit

Lead Followers not only avoid claiming credit but also are generous in lavishing credit upon others. Why? The reason is not to manipulate team members but to promote a culture of appreciation. When everyone knows that good work will be greeted with appreciation, the whole team thrives. By contrast, when good work is unnoticed or, even worse, when the leader claims all the credit, then the team's effort dwindles.

The excellent associate pastor in chapter 12 who said his purpose was to make his senior pastor "look good" was able to make that choice because he functioned on a team in which credit was lavished upon others by that same senior pastor. The whole attitude of the team was to help one another do well and to give appreciation to everyone's efforts.

Lead Followers don't claim the credit; they lavish credit upon others.

Don't Settle

Lead Followers don't settle for the unimportant, the unimaginative, or the mediocre. Among the most interesting letters I have received was a concern expressed by a church member whose pastor seemed always to "settle" for a lack of excellence. The member wrote to me, "Jesus did not agonize in the Garden of Gethsemane just so that we can have potluck suppers at church." That's right! There is nothing wrong with potluck suppers, but surely a congregation needs to be about more important issues than functioning as a nice club.

Lead Followers are persons who lead their group toward a mission that is worthy of the model of Jesus, and they won't settle for less. Sometimes when I visit a congregation, I can see how they have settled for less. I notice a lack of hospitality, a lack of preparation and order, a lack of joy, and an absence of purpose. I go home asking myself, "Is this the best we can do?" Fortunately such experiences are rare. Most of the time I go home from one of my visit with a congregation feeling impressed by the way their leaders have not settled but have dedicated themselves to doing their best.

Lead Followers bring out that best in the entire group because they refuse to settle for less.

Stay Focused

Lead Followers avoid settling for less because they stay focused upon the mission. Lead Followers constantly talk about the mission of their congregation, group, or business. They tell stories to lift up the importance of following the mission. They communicate a commitment to the mission, even while offering and receiving grace for those times our humanity gets in the way of reaching the mission. But always their focus is upon the mission.

Many congregations have adopted so-called mission statements, and that is nice. But the real question is this: do you know your mission, and do you make decisions based upon that mission? If the answer is no, then you may have a mission statement but don't have a mission focus.

Lead Followers stay focused upon the mission.

Don't Give Up

Lead Followers never give up. Even when they fail, even when they are wrong, even when their best efforts fall short, they never give up.

Lead Followers realize that the mission of the group is too important to surrender, and they see mistakes as great learning opportunities. Lead Followers are realistic and know that people sometimes let us down, but they keep recruiting, delegating, affirming, and believing in their people. Lead Followers never accept "no" as the final answer; instead they only hear "not yet" from others and from themselves.

Lead Followers know that following Jesus and other Christian leaders is what helps them become Lead Followers. And they live in the assurance of Jesus, who said, "I myself will be with you every day until the end of this present age" (Matt. 28:20).

An Inquiry from Jesus

"Why did you begin to have doubts?" (Matt. 14:31).

Jesus asks this question of Peter when he begins to sink. Peter had seen Jesus walking on water, and he wanted to follow his leader. His first few steps were going well, until he realized what he was doing and began to sink. Jesus rescued him and asked, "Why do you begin to have doubts?"

The Response of a Lead Follower

Cindy Reynolds is the superintendent of the North District in the Indiana Conference and also a former council director. She also cochaired the Imagine Indiana Team that helped create the new Indiana Conference from the former North and South conferences. Here is her response:

Bishop Coyner has created a simple list of ten practices that, if followed, have the potential to develop skills to be a Lead Follower. A list like this reminds me of the Ten Commandments given as a way to shape life in relationship to God and to God's creation in humanity. The ten simple ways to become a Lead Follower are not just words or rules but are practices that shape a way of life and being. They speak to the way we are to be connected to God, connected to others, and connected to God's mission. In fact, upon deeper reflection, it appears that each of the ten simple ways finds its power in relationship. It is a relationship with God that creates an effective follower who is energized by listening and praying and by putting into perspective the joy in the journey, so that the right questions are asked and the right people are discerned and recruited. It is a relationship with others that brings opportunities to lead by delegating, lavishing credit upon others, setting high standards of excellence, and keeping one another focused on the mission so that no one gives up and together the goal is accomplished. Using the ten simple ways develops healthy relationships and leads to effectiveness for the Lead Follower.

A clear example from my experience on the cabinet in the Indiana Conference is our practice of praying for one another as prayer partners. We have learned that intentional prayer for and with one another strengthens our relationships and keeps us connected to God's mission as we do the ministry of supervision and leadership. We are learning to be Lead Followers by leading and following in a trusting relationship.

Reflect and Discuss

1. Have you ever started to be a leader and then found yourself having doubts?

2. Do you doubt your own ability, the ability of your team who supports you, or the power of God to sustain you?

3. Have you ever avoided difficult situations by choosing to stay in the boat?

4. Does this whole idea of being a Lead Follower sound like something you want to do?

5. Are you going to get out of the boat?

CPSIA information can be obtained at www.ICGtesting.com
Printed in the USA
BVOW06s0856040416

442854BV00019B/131/P